Eight Keys
to Progressive
Spiritual
Development

Darius M. John

Order this book online at www.trafford.com
or email orders@trafford.com

Most Trafford titles are also available at major online book retailers.

Printed in the United States of America.

ISBN: 978-1-4907-0747-1 (sc)
ISBN: 978-1-4907-0746-4 (e)

Trafford rev. 08/23/2013

 www.trafford.com

North America & international
toll-free: 1 888 232 4444 (USA & Canada)
fax: 812 355 4082

CONTENTS

INTRODUCTION

The golden sun was now rising above the horizon. Beams of light traveled in every direction revealing the beauty of a new day. The calm sea like a huge mirror reflected the light of the up coming sun. The morning was greeted by the flattering wings of the birds that danced praises to their creator as they flew by. The morning dew glittered like expensive crystals in the light of the sun. All nature seemed to be in one accord as the gentle breeze created a welcoming atmosphere.

It was still early morning when Jesus was with His disciples by the seaside. As sheep having no shepherd the people began to assemble about Him. There were people from Galilee, Judea, from Jerusalem, Idumea, from beyond Jordan and from Tyre and Sidon—a vast multitude, hearing all the many things that He was doing, came to Him. (Mark 3: 8) Luke gave this account—Jesus came down with them and took His stand on a level spot, with a great crowd of His disciples and a vast throng of people . . . who came to listen to Him and to be cured of their diseases—even those who were disturbed and troubled with unclean spirits, and they were being healed [also]. And all the multitude were seeking to touch Him, for healing power was all the while going forth from Him and curing them all [saving them from severe illness or calamities]. Luke 6: 17-19

The seaside was narrow and those who came to hear Jesus could not have gotten close enough to hear His voice. The Savior led the way up the mountainside and finding a level space that could have accommodated the vast assembly He sat down on the grass and was followed by the disciples and the multitude.

Christ and His disciples were seldom alone when He gathered them to receive His teaching. His audience was not made up only of those who knew the way of life. His mission was to reach the multitude who were in darkness, ignorance and error. His teaching of truth, were given to reach minds that have been enslave by the devil. Jesus, being Himself the Truth, sought to uplift all who came to Him with words of warning, entreaty and encouragement.

The disciples took their place closes to Jesus. Even though the crowd pressed upon Him, the disciples understood that they were to maintain their position in the presence of their master. They were attentive listeners eager to understand the truth and not lose a word of His instruction.

The Sermon on the Mount was given especially to the disciples, yet it was spoken in the hearing of the great multitude. The disciples waited in expectation feeling that something more than usual was about to take place. They believed that the kingdom was soon to be established and assured themselves that an announcement concerning it was about to be made. This feeling of expectancy also pervaded the multitude whose faces gave evidence of their deep interest.

As they sat awaiting the words of the Teacher, their hearts were filled with thoughts of future glory. The Scribed and Pharisees looked for the day when they should have power and authority over the hated Romans. The poor peasants and fishermen hoped to hear assurance that their fear of want, were to be exchanged for a life of plenty and ease. 'In the place of the one coarse garment which was their covering by day and their blanket at night, they hoped that Christ would give them the rich and costly robes of their conquerors.' All hoped that

Israel was soon to be honored above all nations as the chosen of God and Jerusalem exalted to be the head of a universal kingdom.

The hope of worldly greatness was disappointed by Christ. In His Sermon on the Month He sought to whip away the misconceptions that had been developed by false education. He sought to give His hearers the right idea of His kingdom and of His own character. He did not, however, make a direct attack on the errors of the people. He knew too well the misery of the world due to the problem of sin, yet He did not openly expose their wretchedness. The Master Teacher taught them things of grave importance above that which they had known. Without smashing their ideas of the kingdom of God, He taught them the conditions of entrance therein. The truths He taught them are of equal importance to all who follow Him. We need to learn the foundation principles of the kingdom of God.

The first words of Christ to the listening disciple and multitude were words of blessing. This is what He taught them:

> God blesses those who realize their need for Him, for the kingdom of Heaven is given to them.
> God blesses those who mourn, for they will be comforted.
> God blesses those who are gentle and lowly, for the whole earth will belong to them.
> God blesses those who are hungry and thirsty for justice, for they will receive it in full.
> God blesses those who are merciful, for they will be shown mercy.
> God blesses those whose hearts are pure, for they will see God.
> God blesses those who work for peace, for they will be called the children of God.
> God blesses those who are persecuted because they live for God, for the kingdom of heaven is theirs.

God blesses you when you are mocked and persecuted and lied about because you are my followers. Be happy about it! Be very glad! For a great reward awaits you in heaven. And remember, the ancient prophets were persecuted, too. You are the salt of the earth. But what good is salt if it has lost its flavor? Can you make it useful again? It will be thrown out and trampled underfoot as worthless. You are the light of the world—like a city on a mountain, glowing in the night for all to see. Don't hide your light under a basket! Instead, put it on a stand and let it shine for all. In the same way, let your good deeds shine out for all to see, so that everyone will praise your heavenly Father. (Matt. 5: 2-16 NLT)

The word blessed comes from the Greek *"makarioi"* meaning literally happy, fortunate or blissful. Pronouncing a blessing involves proclaiming a divinely conferred sense of well-being which is a foretaste of heaven. It seems that its root is a word meaning great, and originally referred to outward prosperity. As the language evolved the word took on a moral element which raised it "from outward propriety to inward correctness as the essence of happiness." Vincent's Word Studies in the New Testament vol. 1 p.34

In the Old Testament the idea involved in the use of the word learns more to the side of outward prosperity. On the other hand it conveys the idea of inward prosperity in the New Testament. It emphasizes as its primary element a sense of Gods approval based on righteousness which rests ultimately on love for God. Entering the realm of Christian thought the word freed itself from the concept of outward blessedness to become a true symbol of happiness that is identified with pure character. It was this idea of happiness Jesus had in mind when He began His exposition. He linked His teaching to the hopes of His listeners, for their messianic concept was that of deliverance and happiness. His concept of happiness, however, stood in strong contrast with the popular thought of the day. Happiness as viewed by the world consists of what a man possesses—his land and houses, his social position, his intellectual attainment and the other good things of this life. According to Jesus, happiness consist of ones wealth of the inner life—his moral strength, his spiritual insight, in the character one is able to form within himself and in the service he is able to render to his fellowmen. Happiness, therefore, according to Jesus is the by-product of a righteousness life. It is not the object but the fruit of the life.

There are eight blessings or beatitudes in Matthew 5: 3-11 and these can be divided into two groups. The first group shows the secret of inner peace, it is attained as one develops his relationship with God. These personal qualities are (a) poor in spirit—humility (b) mourn—penitence (c) meek—self-control (d) hunger and thirst—deep desire for righteousness. The second group point out the secret of social peace which is developed as one pursues and develops his relationship with his fellowmen. These social qualities are (e) merciful—extending of mercy to others (f) pure in heart—acceptance of and respect for individuals (g) peacemaker—ambassador of peace (h) persecuted—sacrificial service.

The significance of these eight qualities must be viewed and understood not only as separate principles but in the relation of each to the whole. It is of eternal value to apply each one of these principles to the life. They form a "heavenly ladder" by which one can grow into the perfect character God is desirous of developing in His people.

CHAPTER ONE

A NEW INHERITANCE

From the very beginning of man, Satan began his campaign to deceive the human race. He began his rebellion in heaven and has desired to bring all the inhabitants of the earth to unite with him in his warfare against the government of God. Our first parent lived in perfect happiness, walking in obedience to the law of God. There obedience stood as a constant testimony against Satan and his claim that the law of God is oppressive and opposed to His creatures. The beautiful home of Adam and Eve excited the envy of Satan and he determined to cause their fall. Having separated them from God, they were brought under his power and he gained possession of the earth. Satan thus established his kingdom in opposition to the kingdom of God.

Some four thousand years after the fall of man, Paul the apostle wrote as recorded in Romans 3: 23—For all have sinned, and come short of the glory of God. This says literally, "all sinned." The sin of our father Adam marred the divine image of God in man. All, of his descendants continued to fall short and be deprived of the image and glory of God. Sin and death—a principle and power—have passed on to all who participated in the sin of Adam. The participation in Adam's sin is universal, for it spans man in all ages and in all lands. There is no exception—all have sinned. Sin is personified by Paul, he says:

- Sin has reigned in death. Rom. 5: 21
- Sin works death. Rom. 7: 13
- Sin has dominion over us. Rom. 6: 14
- Sin aroused and stimulated all kind of forbidden desires. Rom. 7:8
- Sin deceives, en-trapped, cheated and kills us. Rom. 7: 11

So we see that by the offence of Adam the principle of sin entered our world. Sin then because the source of all offences. By violating the law of God sin was introduced to man. Adam heard the warning of God—"for in the day that you eat of it you shall surely die." (Gen. 2: 17) Now after sin the sentence of God was "for dust you are and to dust you shall return." Gen. 3:19 Amp

A study of the Bible will show that there are three kinds of death:

1. Spiritual death

> And you [He made alive], who were dead (slain) by [your] trespasses and sins. (Eph. 2: 1)
> We know that we have passed over out of death into life by the fact that we love the brethren (our fellow Christians) 1 Jn. 3: 14a
> A life that is lived without a knowledge or a relationship with God is a life that is dead spiritually. All men are dead because of the inheritance of sin. Our only hope is in Jesus who has the power to quicken us and inject His life into us.

2. First or Temporal death

> He said these things, and then added, our friend Lazarus is at rest and sleeping; but I am going there that I may awaken him out of his sleep. The disciples answered, Lord, if he is sleeping, he will recover. However, Jesus had spoken of his death, but they thought that He referred to falling into a refreshing and natural sleep. So then Jesus told them plainly, Lazarus is dead. Jn. 11: 11-14 Amp.

> This is the physical death that all men will experience for the Bible says "the living know that they shall die but the dead knows nothing." Eccl. 9:5 Amp.

3. Second or Eternal death

> ". . . but rather be afraid of Him who can destroy both soul and body in hell" (Gehenna). Matt. 10: 28b

> "He who overcomes (is victorious) shall in no way be injured by the second death". Rev. 2: 11b

> "Blessed and holy is he that hath part in the first resurrection on such the second death hath no power, but they shall be priests of God and of Christ, and shall reign with him a thousand years." Rev. 20: 6 KJV

The sentence of death pronounced upon Adam has passed upon all men. Adam's sentence, however, did not refer to the second death. For the second death cannot be passed on to anyone, it comes as a result of the judgment when every man will be judged according to their works. (Rev. 20: 12-13) In the final judgment of God, the final sentence will be based on individual responsibility, "for He will render to every man according to his works [justly, as his deeds deserve]." (Rom. 2: 6) Amp.

The Bible points out clearly that all men go down to the grave. It is in this that all men share in the penalty of Adam's transgression. By rebelling against God the right to the tree of life was lost to them. This resulted in their death and in passing on this death to their descendants.

"After their sin Adam and Eve were no longer to dwell in Eden. They earnestly entreated that they might remain in the home of their innocence and joy. They confessed that they had forfeited all right to that happy abode, but pledged themselves for the future to yield strict obedience to God. But they were told that their nature had become depraved by sin; they had lessened their strength to resist evil and had opened the way for Satan to gain more ready access to them. In their innocence they had yielded to temptation and now, in a state of conscious guilt, they would have less power to maintain their integrity." Patriarchs and Prophets p. 306

"Thus Adam and Eve passed on to their posterity a tendency to sin and a liability to its punishment, death. By their transgression, sin was introduced as an infectious power in human nature antagonistic to God, and this infection has continued ever since. It is because of this infection of nature, traceable to Adam's sin that men must be born again." SDA Bible Commentary vol. 6 p. 531

On the passing down of a sinful nature from father to son the following should be noted:

> "It is inevitable that children should suffer from the consequences of parental wrongdoing, but they are not punished for the parent's guilt, except as they participate in their sins. It is usually the case, however, that children walk in the steps of their parents. By inheritance and example the sons become partakers of the father's sin. Wrong tendencies, perverted appetites, and debased morals, as well as physical disease and degeneracy, are transmitted as a legacy from father to

son, to the third and fourth generation. This fearful truth should have a solemn power to restrain men from following a course of sin." Patriarchs and Prophets p. 306

In Romans 5, Paul emphasizes the fact that just as sin and death—a principle and power—came through Adam to the whole human family, so righteousness and life as a counteracting and conquering principle and power, come through Jesus Christ to the whole human race. Just as death has been handed down to all men who took part in Adam's sin, so life is passed on to all who take part in the righteousness of Christ.

Adam gave death but Jesus Christ gives life. By His life and death He achieved for the human race more than recovery from the ruin that came through sin. It was the purpose of Satan to bring about the "eternal separation between God and man; but in Christ we become more closely united to God than if we had never fallen." Desire of Ages p. 25

Through Adam the principle of sin was operative in the life. Now, to all who freely and willingly partake of the righteousness of Christ, God implants the principle of the new life in them and making the governing disposition of the soul holy. This doing is totally an act of God and is called regeneration.

Regeneration is needed because man is wretched and lost if left to himself. Religious rites and ceremonial washing could not change the sinful nature of man. Man's only hope is to accept God's solution to the sin problem—a complete reformation of life. The purpose of God is not just to provide forgiveness to men but to restore man to a sinless life. Regeneration is thus the initial step that begins the process of sanctification. "He saves us, not because of any works of righteousness that we had done, but because of His own pity and mercy by [the] cleansing [bath] of the new birth (regeneration) and renewing of the Holy Spirit. (Titus 3: 5) Amp.

On regeneration, Louis Berkhof says: Regeneration is a creative work of God, and is therefore a work in which man is purely passive, and in which there is no place for human cooperation. This is a very important point, since it stresses the fact that salvation is wholly of God. (b) The creative work of God produces a new life, in virtue of which man, made alive with Christ, shares the resurrection life, and can be called a new creature, "created in Christ Jesus for good works, which God afore prepared that we should walk in them," Eph. 2: 10. (c) The two elements must be distinguished in regeneration, namely, generation or the begetting of the new life, and bearing or bringing forth, by which the new life is brought forth out of its hidden depths. Generation implants the principle of the new life in the soul, and the new birth causes this principle to begin to assert itself in actions. This distinction is of great importance for a proper understanding of regeneration. Systematic Theology p 465

In Adam, sin and death was our inheritance but now in Christ Jesus we are regenerated. Christ implants the principle of the new spiritual life in us, thus radically changing the ruling disposition of the soul, which, now guided by the Holy Spirit, gives a new beginning to the life that now moves in the direction dictated by God. This spiritual change affects the whole being.

The intellect

1 Cor. 2: 14-15 states:

> But the natural, non-spiritual man does not accept or welcome or admit into his heart the gifts and teachings and revelation of the Spirit of God, for they are folly (meaningless nonsense) to him; and he is incapable of knowing them [of progressively recognizing, understanding, and becoming better acquainted with them] because they are spiritually discerned and estimated and appreciated.
>
> But the spiritual man tries all things [he examines, investigates, inquires into, questions, and discerns all

things], yet is himself to be put on trial and judged by no one [he can read the meaning of everything, but no one can properly discern or appraise or get an insight into him]. Amp.

2 Cor. 4: 6 says:

"For God, who commanded the light to shine out of darkness, hath shined in our hearts to give the light of the knowledge of the glory of God in the face of Jesus Christ." KJV

Colossians 3: 10 says:

"And have put on the new man, which is renewed in knowledge after the image of him that created him." KJV

The Will

Philippians 2: 13 shows:

[Not in your own strength] for it is God who is all the while effectually at work in you [energizing and creating in you the power and desire], both to will and to work for His good pleasure and satisfaction and delight. Amp.

Hebrews 13: 21 states:

Strengthen (complete, perfect) and make you what you ought to be and equip you with everything good that you may carry out His will; [while He Himself]

works in you and accomplishes that which is pleasing in His sight, through Jesus Christ (the Messiah); to whom be the glory forever and ever (to the ages of the age). Amen (so be it).

The Feelings and Emotions

Matthew 5: 4 says:

> "Blessed are they that mourn; for they shall be comforted."

1 Peter 1: 8 shows:

> Without having seen Him, you love Him; though you do not [even] now see Him, you believe in Him and exult and thrill with inexpressible and glorious (triumphant, heavenly) joy. Amp.

Regeneration then, is an instantaneous change of nature, affecting the whole being, intellectually, emotionally and morally. This change is not a gradual process like the process of sanctification. It is instant and begins the new life in Christ. It must be noted, however, that after the act of regeneration is performed by God, the believer has to cooperate with the working of the Holy Spirit to run with patience the Christian race that is set before him.

Hebrews 12: 1 says:

> . . . let us strip off and throw aside every encumbrance (unnecessary weight) and that sin which so readily (deftly and cleverly) clings to and entangles us, and let us run with patient endurance and steady

active persistence the appointed course of the race that
is set before us. Amp.

One who is motivated by faith will not hold back on getting rid
of any and everything that might keep him from achieving his goal. In
the Christian race, everyone may win, for the competition is not with
others but with oneself. It is not required to out-do what someone else
has done. The only requirement is to exercise faithfulness and patience
and through the grace of Christ, overcome every weight—every
tendency to evil.

"Every man has some besetting sin, some tendency to evil that
seeks to impede him as he runs the race. When he gains the victory
over that particular evil propensity, another takes its place and presses
for the mastery. Thus the pathway of salvation is beset by one battle
after another. But it is every Christian's privilege to achieve victory each
step of the way. Whatever may be the sin that so easily besets us we are
to lay it aside like an ancient runner laying aside his flowing robes and
girding himself for the race." SDA Bible Commentary vol. 7 p. 481

Understanding that the Christian race is a lifelong experience, the
born again child of God is called to have "patience and perseverance—
perseverance in the face of successive difficulties and disappointment
and patience to await the reward at the end of the course." Ibid 481

The counsel of Paul to the Philippians is relevant here—work out
(cultivate, carry out to the goal, and fully complete) your own salvation
with reverence and awe and trembling (self-distrust, with serious
caution, tenderness of conscience, watchfulness against temptation,
timidly shrinking from whatever might offend God and discredit the
name of Christ). Phil. 2: 12 Amp.

Paul calls on the believers to carry out to completion the work
which God has begun in them. The Scriptures teach clearly that each
individual must cooperate with the will and power of God. We all
must strive to enter in (Luke 13: 24), put off the old man (Col. 3: 9),

lay aside every weight, run with patience (Heb. 12: 1), resist the devil (James 4: 7), and endure unto the end (Matt. 24: 13).

Do not be mistaken, salvation is not of works, but it must be worked out. It originates from the mediation of Christ alone, but has to be lived out by personal individual cooperation. We must always be conscious of our personal obligation to daily live by the grace of God, a life consistent with the principles of Heaven.

Jesus opens up the dynamics of regeneration in His encounter with Nicodemus who secretly sought Him by night. "Jesus answered and said unto him, verily, verily, I say unto thee, except a man be born again, he cannot see the kingdom of God." John 3:3

"According to Jewish theology, to be born a son of Abraham was almost certain a guarantee of admission into the kingdom of heaven (ch. 8: 33). But in order to be saved, non-Jews must become sons of Abraham by adoption. It would not have startled Nicodemus to hear Jesus affirm that non-Jews must be "born again" in order to "see the kingdom of God," but the idea that he, a circumspect Jew, stood outside the circle of salvation was a new and disturbing thought. Two and a half years later (ch. 8: 39) Jesus explicitly declared that descent from Abraham is to be reckoned by moral likeness rather than by physical relationship." SDA Bible Commentary vol. 5 p. 927

Certainly Nicodemus understood that Jesus was not speaking of physically being born again. In his response to Jesus, he acknowledges the impossibility by asking two questions. "How can a man be born when he is old? Can he enter the second time into his mother's womb, and be born? He could not readily accept the words of Jesus that, he, a devout Jew needed to be born again.

It is of vital importance to grasp the words of Jesus when He said "That which is born of the flesh is flesh, and that which is born of the spirit is spirit." John 3:6. The principle that all living things reproduce after its kind is relevant here. Everyone that is born of the Spirit is liken to the wind. The new birth is invisible. It cannot be seen by the natural eye in the same way the wind cannot be seen. Just as the effects of the wind can be seen, so the effects of the new birth can be seen in the fruit produced.

Nicodemus "knowledge of salvation was only theoretical, and was based on a false theory at that. If Nicodemus had experienced the new birth, he would not only understand it himself, but be able to speak intelligently of it to others." Ibid. 928

Elementary to a relationship with God is the experience of regeneration or being born again. This gives access to the kingdom of divine grace. One cannot see or even enter His kingdom apart from having this encounter.

Remembering that regeneration is an act of God that He performs in our hearts, we have nothing to boast about. In acknowledgement of His undying love that He graciously bestows on us, we will cry out like Saul on the road of Damascus "Lord, what will you have me do?" Acts 9: 6

Being born again is the first step or stage of spiritual life. Growth must begin to take place. As new born babies the steps will be small, progress will be slow, but every forward movement count in pressing toward the prize of the high calling in Jesus Christ. Realizing that this is a spiritual journey, it will end in massive failure if we neglect to understand our true spiritual condition. Jesus said: "Blessed are the poor in spirit, for theirs is the kingdom of heaven." Matthew 5: 3

CHAPTER TWO

---•---

DISCOVER YOUR TRUE SELF

Key 1

Recognition of ones true spiritual poverty and the
need for redemption

It has been ordained by God that the gospel be preached to the spiritually poor. It is not received by the spiritually proud, for they see themselves as religiously right having need of nothing. There has been one fountain created for the washing away of sin, and this can only be access by the poor in spirit, those who are humble and contrite. There is nothing the Lord can do for the recovery of an individual until he becomes convinced of his own weakness, peals away all self-sufficiency and yields himself to the control of God. Only then can he receive the gift of heaven which is reserved for those who acknowledge their need. They shall have unrestricted access to Him in whom all fullness dwells.

For thus saith the high and lofty one that inhabiteth eternity, whose name is Holy; I dwell in the high and holy place, with him also that is of a contrite and humble spirit, to revive the spirit of the humble, and to revive the heart of the contrite ones. Isaiah 57: 15

At an elevation of about 800 ft. above sea level some 100 miles east of Ephesus was Laodicea. It is believed to be founded by Antiochus II (261-246 B.C.) who was one of the Seleucid rulers of the Hellenistic era. He named the city after Laodicea, his sister and wife and populated it with Syrians and Jews take from Babylonia. In the first century of its existence Laodicea was just another town, but this rapidly changed after the formation of the Roman province of Asia in 2nd century B.C.

Laodicea became the trade center for glossy black wool and black garments which was locally manufactured. These items were exported to many countries. The city also became known as an export center for its popular Phrygian eye powder, and as a financial center with several banks that attracted much wealth. A well-known school of medicine located at the temple of Men Karou added to the ame of this growing city.

Laodicea came to be known as one of the richest cities of the East. In A.D. 60 a severe earthquake destroyed this wealthy city. Emperor Nero offered financial help for reconstruction but the proud and wealthy citizens refused his aid telling him that they had enough resources to rebuild their city without assistance from outside. Nero then called it "one of the illustrious cities of Asia."

The Laodicea's felt that they were "rich and increased with goods" and had "need of nothing," which in reality they were in spiritual trouble. They were "wretched and miserable and poor." They were called by the Lord not to trust in their banks filled with gold but to buy of Him gold tried in the fire, that they may be truly rich. He pointed them away from their fine black garments to buy of Him white raiment's that they may be clothed so that the shame of their nakedness be not seen.

It is easy to become proud and lifted up because of the success of your hands. All around us we see the separation or the different classes of people—upper class, middle class and lower class; those above the poverty line and those below the poverty line; those who live in the ghetto, in the suburbs, in the areas where only the "who's who" lives and the list goes on. This author is not against success. He believes that every man has the ability to be successful. The use of this ability, however, will determine whether one is successful or not.

The Laodiceans were wealthy in this world's goods but were lacking in the area of their lives that truly counts. They were spiritually bankrupt. Their lives were spent in acquiring earthly wealth that is perishable at the neglect of that which is eternal. Wealth and riches are of benefit in this life only; building spiritual wealth is not only for this life, but for eternity. It is necessary to point out that one must have the right attitude toward life and the things he accomplishes in this life. The silver and gold will all perish, but the character that is built according to the principles of God's word will last throughout eternity.

In His first blessing the Savior deals with the attitude we hold to in dealing with money, our fellow men and with God. He says that those who are poor in spirit shall be blessed.

"And he sat down next to the treasury and saw how the crowd was casting money into the treasury. Many rich [people] were throwing in large sums.

And a woman who was poverty-stricken came and put in two copper mites [the smallest of coins] which together make half of a cent.

And he called his disciples [to him] and said to them, "Truly and surely I tell you, this widow, [she who is] poverty-stricken, has put in more than all those contributing to the treasury.

For they all threw in out of their abundance; but she, out of her deep poverty, has put in everything that she had—[even] all she had on which "to live." Mark 12:41-44

This poverty-stricken woman lived in extreme want. She lived hand-to-mouth, working today in order to have food tomorrow. Most likely she lived her life not knowing where the next meal was coming from. Having nothing but two copper coins she cast in "all of her living" into the treasury. Her gift was given from her heart that was overflowing with love for God.

"Many of the rich brought large sums, which they presented with great ostentation. Jesus looked upon them sadly, but made no comment on their liberal offerings. Presently His countenance lighted as He saw a poor widow approach hesitatingly, as though fearful of being observed. As the rich and haughty swept by, to deposit their offerings, she shrank back as if hardly daring to venture farther. And yet she longed to do something, little though it might be, for the cause she loved. She looked at the gift in her hand. It was very small in comparison with the gifts of those around her, yet it was her all. Watching her opportunity, she hurriedly threw in her two mites, and turned to hasten away. But in doing this she caught the eyes of Jesus, which was fastened earnestly upon her . . ."

"Then His words of commendation fell on her ear; "this poor widow hath cast in more than they all." Tears of joy filled her eyes as she felt that her act was understood and appreciated! "Her heart went with her gift; its value was estimated, not by the worth of the coin, but by the love to God and the interest in His work that had prompted the deed." Desire of the Ages p. 356

On one occasion Jesus went back to Nazareth where he grew up, there He entered the synagogue as He normally did on the Sabbath. Being invited to read, the writing of the prophet Isaiah was handed to Him. He found where it was written:

> The Spirit of the Lord [is] upon Me, because He has anointed Me [the Anointed One, the Messiah] to preach the good news (The Gospel) to the poor; He has sent Me to announce release to the captives and recovery of sight to the blind, to send forth as delivered those who are oppressed [who are downtrodden, bruised, crushed, and broken down by calamity, to proclaim the accepted and acceptable year of the Lord [the day when salvation and the free favor of God profusely abound]. Luke 4: 18,19 Amp.

Now as He sat on some unknown mountain in Galilee, He began to teach the multitude not of poverty in terms of dollars and cents but of poverty of the Spirit. He said to them "Blessed are the poor in Spirit; for theirs is the kingdom of heaven." Matthew 5:3

These powerful words fell on the multitude ears as strange and new teaching. His sayings were contrary to all they have been taught by the priest or rabbi. He taught with a power that held them spellbound. As divine love flowed from Him all felt instinctively that he was one who can read the secrets of their soul. Yet He came near to them with tender compassion. As they listened, the Holy Spirit revealed to their open hearts the meaning of the lesson they so much needed to learn.

It was the disciple Peter, when he saw the divine power of Jesus in the miraculous draft of fishes, who carried out and fell at the feet of the Saviour, "depart from me, for I am a sinful man, O Lord" (Luke 5:8). In the same way there were those in the multitude upon the mount who in the presence of His purity felt their nothingness and longed for the grace of God.—"wretched, miserable, poor, blind, and naked" (Rev. 3:17); they longed for "the grace of God that bringeth salvation. (Titus 2:11).

"The poor were usually at the mercy of unscrupulous officials, businessmen, and neighbors. Further, it was generally supposed that the suffering of poverty was due to the curse of God—that their unfortunate state was their own fault. Few felt sympathetic toward them in their unhappy plight . . . Those who have little of this world's goods are frequently conscious of their needs and of their reliance upon God and thus frequently susceptible to the preaching of the gospel. The gospel of Jesus means relief for the poor, light for the ignorant, alleviation of distress for the suffering, and emancipation for the slaves of sin." SDA Bible Commentary vol. 8 p. 728

The consciousness of one's spiritual destitution is needed before one can enter into the Kingdom of God. This sense of need is the first condition of entrance into His kingdom of grace. The work to relieve this spiritual condition can never be effected by our own efforts. It can only be accomplished by and through the mercy of God.

For it is by free grace (God's unmerited favor) that you are saved (delivered from judgment and made partakers of Christ's salvation) through [your] faith. And this [salvation] is not yourselves [of your own doing, it came not through your own striving], but it is the gift of God; not because of works [not the fulfillment of the Law's demands], lest any man should boast. [It is not the result of what anyone can possibly do, so no one can pride himself in it or take glory to himself.] Eph. 2:8, 9 Amp.

In the time of Christ the religious leaders felt that they were rich in spiritual goods. The prayer of the Pharisee expressed the felling of the entire nation. He also told this parable to some people who trusted in themselves and were confident that they were righteous [that they were upright and in right standing with God] and scorned and made nothing of all the rest of men:

> Two men went up into the temple [enclosure] to pray, the one a Pharisee and the other a tax collector. The Pharisee took his stand ostentatiously and began to pray thus before and with himself. God, I thank you that I am not like the rest of men—extortioners (robbers), swindlers [unrighteous in heart and life], adulterers—or even like this tax collector here. I fast twice a week; I give tithes of all that I gain.
>
> But the tax collector [merely] standing at a distance, would not even lift up his eyes to heaven, but kept striking his breast, saying, O God, be favorable (be gracious, be merciful) to me, the especially wicked sinner that I am! I tell you this man went down to his home justified (forgiven and made upright and in right standing with God), rather than the other man; for everyone who exalts himself will be humbled, but he who humbles himself will be exalted. Luke 18:9-14 Amp.
>
> "It was through consciousness of his own spiritual poverty that the publican in the parable "went down to his home justified" rather than the self-righteous Pharisee." "There is no room in the kingdom of heaven for the proud, the self-satisfied, and the self-righteous. Christ bids the poor in heart to exchange their poverty for the riches of His grace." SDA Bible Commentary vol. 5 p. 325

The poor in spirit then will have a humble opinion of himself. He will accept that he is who he is—saved and secured in Jesus only because of the grace of God.

Paul points out:

> For by the grace (unmerited favor of God) given to me I warn everyone among you not to estimate and think of himself more highly than he ought [not to have an exaggerated opinion of his own importance], but to rate his ability with sober judgment, each according to the degree of faith apportioned by God to him. Rom. 12:3 Amp.

The poor in spirit knows and accepts the fact that he is not superior, better than, more important than, more valuable than, more holy than, more righteous than any other human being and that before God he is spiritually dead. His attitude toward others will not be overbearing, haughty or proud. He will view each person as valuable to life with gifts, talents and abilities to make a contribution to society and to the world. He acknowledges that each life has a given purpose to fulfill and it is part of the whole. I will live life in humility and with appreciation.

The poor in spirit will recognize that he is a sinner and that he has no righteousness of his own.

> "Since all have sinned and are falling short of the honor and glory which God bestows and receives." Rom. 3:23 Amp.
>
> "Well then, are we [Jews] superior and better off than they? No, not at all. We have already charged that all men, both Jews and Greeks (Gentiles), are under sin [held down by and subject to its power and control].

As it is written, "none is righteous, just and truthful and upright and conscientious, no not one." Rom. 3:9, 10

On account of these biblical truths, the poor in spirit will acknowledge his utter helplessness before God and recognize that he is totally dependent upon his heavenly father to meet his every need. He sees the reality of his true condition, accepts that something is wrong with him and is driven to look beyond himself to God who is the fountain of healing and life and light.

Looking outside of himself, he becomes aware that no man is worthy to give the help that he stands in need of. He understands that he can be saved only by the rich grace and mercy of God. "For by grace [alone] are you saved through faith." He becomes eager to stand where God places him; to go wherever he is sent; to accept whatever cross is placed on him and to make the ultimate sacrifice if called upon to do so. All control having been yielded to God, he now stands willing to be a channel to be used for honor and glory.

> [Not in your own strength] for it is God who is all the while effectually at work in you [energizing and creating in you the power and desire], both to will and to work for His good pleasure and satisfaction and delight. Phil. 2:13

Noted that it is God who is working in us, in order for Him to do His bidding in us, we must surrender to Him giving Him permission and control. Isaiah beholding a vision from God had this to say:

> In the year that King Uzziah died, [in a vision] I saw the Lord sitting upon a throne, high and lifted up, and the skirts of His train filled the [most holy part of the] temple.

Above Him stood the Seraphim; each had six wings: with two [each] covered his [own] face, and with two [each] covered his feet, and two [each] flew. And one cried to another and said, Holy, holy, holy is the Lord of hosts; the whole earth is full of His glory!

And the foundation of the thresholds shook at the voice of him who cried, and the house was filled with smoke.

Then said I, woe is me! For I am undone and ruined, because I am a man of unclean lips, and I dwell in the midst of a people of unclean lips; for my eyes have seen the King, the Lord of hosts!

Then flew one of the seraphim [heavenly beings] to me, having a live coal in his hand which he had taken with tongs from the altar; and with it he touched my mouth and said, "Behold, this has touched your lips; your iniquity and guilt are taken away, and your sin is completely atoned for and forgiven."

Also I heard the voice of the Lord, saying, "Whom shall I send? And who will go for us?" Then said I, "Here am I; send me." Isa. 6:1-8 Amp.

We need here to underscore some important points:

1. God revealed His attribute—perfect holiness of character.

    The angels being impressed with the holiness of God cried with melodious voices holy, holy, holy.

2. God's unspoken message to the prophet.

    God here seeks to engrave upon the mind of Isaiah a concept of His holiness, so that in return he can keep this attribute of the divine before the people that they may be encouraged to put behind them their sins and press toward holiness.

3. Self evaluation of the prophet—"woe is me."

In chapter 5 the prophet Isaiah had been announcing woes upon God's people because of their sins. Now he stands in the very presence of the Almighty God. He becomes aware of the imperfection of his own character. Thus he is driven to cry out "woe is me! For I am undone and ruined."

4. Having a glimpse of God's glory changes everything. Seeing the glory and holiness of God, Isaiah recognizes the sinfulness of mankind. He became aware of his own unworthiness and nothingness as it stands in comparison to the Lord of hosts.

5. Being touched with holy fire,

"The coal from the altar represented the purifying and refining power of divine grace. It signified, as well, a transformation of character. Henceforth, the one great desire of Isaiah for his people was that they too might experience the same work of cleansing and transformation." SDA Bible Commentary vol. 4 p. 129

6. After cleansing comes empowerment for service.

The response of Isaiah was immediate "Here am I, send me." The sinners in Israel were in danger of the Judgment of God that was soon to fall. The prophet longed to see them turn away from their sins, accept the message of hope that he was presenting from God. He desired that his people like himself will catch a vision of the holiness of God and be saved.

7. Today, we all need an experience with God.

> "Jesus had presented the cup of blessing to those who felt that they were "rich and increased with goods" (Rev. 3:17), and had need of nothing, and they had turned with scorn from the gracious gift. He who feels whole, who thinks that he is reasonably good and is contented with his condition, does not seek to become a partaker of the grace and righteousness of Christ. Pride feels no need, and so it closes the heart against Christ and the infinite blessing. He came to give. There is no room for Jesus in the heart of such a person. Those who are rich and honorable in their own eyes do not ask in faith, and receive the blessing of God. They feel that they are full, therefore, they go away empty. Those who know that they cannot possibly save themselves, or of themselves do any righteous action, are the ones who appreciate the help that Christ can bestow. They are the poor in spirit, whom He declares to be blessed." Thoughts From the Mount of Blessing p. 8

It is the work of the Holy Spirit of God to convince men of sin. When the heart becomes moved by His convicting power, man will see that there is absolutely nothing good in himself. He sees that all he has ever done is mixed with sin and selfishness. Like the publican he will pray "God, be merciful to me the sinner." Luke 18:13 Such is the man Christ first makes repentant, then He gives pardon.

Forgiveness is available for those who are sorrowful for their sins, for Jesus is the "Lamb of God, which takes away the sin of the world." John 1:29. The promise of God is:

> "Come now, and let us reason together, says the Lord. Though your sins are like scarlet, they shall be as white as snow; though they are red like crimson, they shall be like wool." Isa. 1:18 Amp

Ezekiel 36:26, 27 states:

> A new heart will I give you and a new spirit will I put within you, and I will take away the stony heart out of your flesh and give you a heart of flesh. And I will put my Spirit within you and cause you to walk in My statutes, and you shall heed My ordinances and do them. (Amp.)
>
> When we draw close to God we will see our own imperfection. The more beauty we see in Him, is the more we will be aware of our true state. Your greatest—my greatest—our greatest need today is to have lips that have been touched with holy fire from the altar of God.

This whole experience begins by being poor in spirit.

The main objective of God's kingdom that must be entered through grace is to restore the happiness of Eden to the hearts of men. All those who enter will experience inward joy and peace. Happiness will come only to those who have peace with God.

Jesus begins his teaching with the promise of happiness. His concept of happiness however, stood in strong contrast with the popular thought. Happiness as the world sees it consists of what a man possesses—his houses and lands, social position, intellectual attainments and the other good things of his life. Jesus is saying on the other hand, that happiness consists of wealth of the inner life—moral strength, spiritual insight, the character from within and the service that is rendered to our fellow men.

The poor in spirit are pronounced blessed for "theirs is the Kingdom of heaven." Christ was here speaking primarily of the present Kingdom of divine grace and secondarily of His future Kingdom of glory. This Kingdom of grace that Christ established is the spiritual kingdom of His love, His grace, and His righteousness. This Kingdom begins in the hearts of men, it flows throughout their lives, and spreads into the hearts and lives of other men with the energizing power of love.

The poor in spirit are blessed now because the kingdom belongs to them right now. They begin to experience the kingdom right now by having access to it through their relationships with heaven.

> Jesus answered, "If a person [really] loves Me, he will keep My word [obey My teaching]; and My Father will love Him, and We will come to him and make our home (abode, special dwelling place) with him. John 14:23 Amp.

It is important to note the promise of Jesus—"We will come."

> The plural emphasizes the oneness of the Father and the Son. They "come," here, to dwell mystically in the heart of the believer. Thus there is a oneness not only between the Father and the Son, but between the Father, the Son, and the believer." SDA Bible Commentary vol. 5 p. 1038

RELATIONSHIP WITH THE FATHER

The poor in spirit have a relationship with God the Father through faith in Jesus Christ.

"For all who are led by the Spirit of God are sons of God." Rom. 8:14 Amp.

For [the Spirit which] you have now received [is] not a spirit of slavery to put you once more in bondage to fear, but you have received the Spirit of adoption [the spirit producing sonship] in [the bliss of] which we cry, Abba [Father]! Rom. 8:15 Amp.

The Spirit Himself [thus] testifies together with our own spirit, [assuring us] that we are children of God. Rom. 8:16 Amp.

And if we are [His] heirs also; heirs of God and fellow heirs with Christ [sharing His inheritance with Him]; only we must share His suffering if we are to share His glory. Rom. 8:17 Amp.

May blessing (praise, laudation, and eulogy) be to the God and Father of our Lord Jesus Christ (the Messiah) who has blessed us in Christ with every spiritual (given by the Holy Spirit) blessing in the heavenly realm! Eph. 1:3 Amp.

But we, brethren beloved by the Lord, ought and are obligated [as those who are in debt] to give thanks always to God for you, because God chose you from the beginning as His first-fruit (first converts) for salvation through the sanctifying work of the [Holy] Spirit and [your] belief in (adherence to, trust in, and reliance on) the Truth. 2 Thess. 2:13 Amp.

RELATIONSHIP WITH THE SON—JESUS CHRIST

But he who enters by the door is the shepherd of the sheep.

The watchman opens the door for this man, and the sheep listen to his voice and heed it; and he calls his own sheep by name and brings (leads) them out.

When he has brought his own sheep outside, he walks on before them, and the sheep follow him because they know his voice.

They will never [on any account] follow a stranger, but will run away from him because they do not know the voice of strangers or recognize their call. John 10:3-5 Amp.

Jesus—the Son provides redemption and restoration to all who come onto Him.

"Through Christ, restoration as well as, reconciliation is provided for man."

"The gulf that was made by sin has been spanned by the cross of Calvary."

"A full, complete ransom has been paid by Jesus, by virtue of which the sinner in pardoned, and the justice of the law is maintained."

"All who believe that Christ is the atoning sacrifice may come and receive pardon for their sins; for through the merit of Christ communication has been opened between God and man."

"God can accept me as His child, and I can claim Him and rejoice in Him as my loving Father."

"We must center our hopes of heaven upon Christ alone, because He is our substitute and surety."

"We have transgressed the law of God, and by the deeds of the law shall no flesh be justified. The best efforts that man in his own strength can make, are valueless to meet the holy and just law that he has transgressed; but through faith in Christ he may claim the righteousness of the Son of God as all sufficient.

"Christ satisfied the demands of the law in His human nature.

"He bore the curse of the law for the sinner, made an atonement for him, that whosoever believeth in Him should not perish, but have everlasting life."

"Genuine faith appropriates the righteousness of Christ, and the sinner is made an overcomer with Christ; for he is made a partaker of the divine nature, and thus divinity and humanity are combined."

"He who is trying to reach heaven by his own works in keeping the law, is attempting an impossibility."

"Man cannot be saved without obedience, but his works should not be of himself; Christ should work in him to will and to do of His good pleasure."
—Review and Herald, July 1, 1890

Let us review the work of Jesus Christ for us that has made our relationship with him possible.

- As a sinner when I come to Jesus, He provides restoration that is both full and complete. Christ's atoning sacrifice on the cross of Calvary provided reconciliation with God and restoration to Adam's state before he sinned.
- The separation that sin created between God and myself has been bridged by the cross.

- By taking my place Christ became my substitute and ransomed me from condemnation and death. He has forgiven me of all my sins yet maintaining the justice of God's holy law.
- Christ opened communication to God so that I can come to Him and receive forgiveness, cleansing and salvation. This has been made possible by His atoning sacrifice.
- Christ and Christ alone became my substitute and surety. There is, therefore, no other name or way that I can be saved.
- Through faith in Christ, I can claim His righteousness as sufficient. I can never be justified by the deeds of the law.
- Through the righteousness of Christ I have been made an overcomer and have become a partaker of His divine nature.
- I cannot obey God in my own strength. I obey because Christ's obedience is working in and through me, causing me to will and to do of His good pleasure.

JESUS THE SON—IMPUTES THEN IMPARTS HIS RIGHTEOUSNESS

"The righteousness by which we are justified is imputed. The righteous by which we are sanctified is imparted. The first is our title to heaven; the second is our fitness for heaven." Review and Herald, June 4, 1895

Let us examine four important terms:

1. Imputed—To attribute, to credit
2. Justify—To declare free of blame; to demonstrate to be just, right, or valid.

When the sinner accepts Jesus, he is justified—Christ forgives him of all his sins and makes him right with God. Christ then takes His own righteousness and credits it to the one who is justified. Now the old sinner stands before God a new creature.

3. Impart—To grant a share of; bestow. To make known; disclose.
4. Sanctify—To set apart for sacred use; consecrate. To make holy; purify.

The new creature is then sanctified—set apart for use, is consecrated to God and begin to live for the glory of God. This cannot be done in his strength for he has none. It can only be done through the righteousness of Christ which is imparted—bestowed or he is allowed to share in so that he can now walk in obedience to the will of God.

Daniel stated, "Imputed righteousness, by which man is justified from guilt, is the foundation upon which imparted righteousness is bestowed, which sanctifies the life conduct, and provides "our fitness for heaven."

"Christ has become our sacrifice and surety. He has become sin for us, that we might become the righteousness of God in Him. Through faith in His name, He imputes unto us His righteousness, and it becomes a living principle in our lives."—Review and Herald, July 12, 1892.

"No repentance is genuine that does not work reformation. The righteousness of Christ is not a cloak to cover unconfessed and unforsaken sin; it is a principle of life that transforms the character and controls the conduct. Holiness is wholeness for God; it is the entire surrender of heart and life to the indwelling of the principles of heaven." The Desire of Ages, p. 555

"Christ imputes to us His sinless character, and presents us to the Father in His own purity. There are many who think that it is impossible to escape from the power of sin, but the promise is that we may be filled with all the fullness of God. We aim too low. The mark is much higher. R&H, July 12, 1892.

"In the religion of Christ there is a regenerating influence that transforms the entire being, lifting man above every debasing, groveling vice, and raising the thoughts and desires toward God and heaven. Linked to the Infinite One, man is made a partaker of the divine nature. Upon him the shafts of evil have no effect; for he is clothed with the panoply of Christ's righteousness." Counsels to Teachers, p. 51, 52

"When the soul surrenders itself to Christ, a new power takes possession of the new heart. A change is wrought which man can never accomplish for himself. It is supernatural work, bringing a super-natural element into human nature. The soul that is yielded to Christ, becomes His own fortress, which he holds in a revolted world, and he intends that no authority shall be known in it but His own. A soul thus kept in possession by the heavenly agencies, is impregnable to the assaults of Satan. But unless we do yield ourselves to the control of Christ, we shall be dominated by the wicked one. We must inevitably be under the control of the one or the other of the two great powers that are contending for the supremacy of the world.

"It is not necessary for us deliberately to choose the service of the kingdom of darkness in order to come under its dominion. We have only to neglect to ally ourselves with the kingdom of light. If we do not co-operate with the heavenly agencies, Satan will take possession of the heart, and will make it his abiding place. The only defense against evil is the indwelling of Christ in the heart through faith in His righteousness. Unless we become vitally connected with God, we can never resist the unhallowed effects of self-love, self-indulgence, and temptation to sin. We may leave off many bad habits, for the time we may part company with Satan; but without a vital connection with God, through the surrender of ourselves to Him moment by moment, we shall be overcome. Without a personal acquaintance with Christ, and a continual communion we are at the mercy of the enemy, and shall do his bidding in the end." The Desire of the Ages, p. 323, 324

To you who have a deep sense of your spiritual poverty, you who feel that you have nothing good in yourself, righteousness and strength can be found by looking unto Jesus.

Do you acknowledge your deep spiritual poverty? Do you recognize that there is nothing good in you? Righteousness and strength may be found in looking unto Jesus. He says, "Come unto Me, all you who labor and are heavy-laden and overburdened and I will cause you to rest. [I will ease and relieve and refresh your souls.] Matt. 11:28

Jesus invites you, come to Me, exchange your poverty for the riches of His grace. None, no not one is worthy of the love of God, save Christ who became our surety. He is worthy and is able to save all who come unto Him. Whatever your past experience have been, however, discouraging your past or present circumstances, if you will come to Jesus now, just as you are, your compassionate Saviour will accept you, He will cover you with His robe of righteousness. He will present you to the Father clothed in the white garment of His own character.

Jesus Christ your Saviour, "is able to keep you without stumbling or slipping or falling, and to present [you] unblemished (blameless and faultless) before the presence of His glory in triumphant joy and exultation [with unspeakable and ecstatic delight]. Jude 24

The poor in spirit becomes uncomfortable and dissatisfied with his spiritual condition. He becomes conscious of the sinfulness of his sin and the high price it cost God to provide forgiveness—the life of His only Son. He is then driven to mourn with a broken heart as he beholds Christ in His beauty and glory.

CHAPTER THREE

GENUINE SORROW AND RENUNCIATION

Key 2

Genuine sorrow for sin, express in mourning.

As the Holy Spirit reveals to the understanding how much our sins have grieved the Saviour, He brings us in contrition to the foot of the cross. By our sins we have wounded afresh our Redeemer, and as we look upon Him we mourn for the sins that have brought aguish upon Him. Such mourning will lead to the renunciation of sin.

Blessed are they that mourn; for they shall be comforted. Matt. 5:4

The English word "mourn" comes from the Greek word denoting intense mourning or to have a broken heart. It is revealing a grief so deep and heavy that it cannot be hidden.

The mourning presented here demonstrates true heart sorry for sin. It was Jesus himself who said, "And I if and when I am lifted up from the earth [on the cross], will draw and attract all men [Gentiles as well as Jews] to Myself." John 12:32 As one takes a look at Jesus uplifted on the cross, he becomes aware of the sinfulness of himself and the rest of humanity. He see that it is sin that afflicted and crucified the Son of God. He recognizes the pure tender love of God that has been extended to him even when he was in total rebellion. His heart is now broken for he has forsaken the Friend who *sticks closer than a brother.* The free gift from heaven he has abused and rejected. He has crucified to himself the Son of God. He acknowledges that he is separated from God by a gulf of sin that he has created. He now mourns in brokenness of heart.

This intense mourning is an outgrowth of one's profound spiritual poverty. It is produced because of the imperfections one sees in his own life. He has acknowledged his spiritual poverty and has become sensitive to his personal unworthiness. There is a relationship here between poor in spirit and this type of mourning. If one fails to acknowledge his spiritual poverty he will be insensitive and dead to his personal unworthiness. In this state there will be no purpose for mourning, for such individuals see themselves as all right, having no need or desire for that which comes from above.

There is a holy standard of perfection that Christ has invited all to reach, but only those who are in poverty of spirit will long for and strive to attain the requirements of heaven. God will hear and respond to the mourning that comes from a broken heart.

The one who mourns because of his own sin will also weep in sympathy with the world and in sorrow for its sin. This type of mourning is selfless because its focus is on others. In this we find Jesus for he was a Man of Sorrow and acquainted with grief. He endured the anguish more than any human language could adequately express. His spirit sunk and was bruised by the sins of men. He worked to remove the wants and the woes of His fellowmen. His heart became heavy with sorrow as He saw humanity neglect to come to Him that they might have life.

All who follow Christ will share in His experiences. As they share in His love they will also enter into His work for the saving of those who are lost. They partake in the suffering of Christ now, and will also share in the glory when it shall be revealed. They have become one with Him in His work, they drink in His cup of sorrow and have become partakers of His joy.

It is because of His suffering that Jesus gained the ministry of consolation—comfort. "In all their [humanity] affliction He was afflicted, . . . in His love and in His pity He redeemed them; and He lifted them up and carried them . . . ." Isaiah 63:9

Hebrews 2:18 says:

> For because He Himself [in His humanity] has suffered in being tempted (tested and tried), He is able [immediately] to run to the cry of (assist, relieve) those who are being tempted and tested and tried [and who therefore are being exposed to suffering]. Amp

To those who mourn, the Lord gives abundance of His grace to melt hearts and to win souls for Him. His love reaches into the souls that are bruised and wounded and becomes a balm of healing to those who are sorrowing.

2 Corinthians 1:3, 4 says:

> Blessed be the God and Father of our Lord Jesus Christ the Father of Sympathy (pity and mercy) and the God [who is the source] of every comfort (consolation and encouragement). Who comforts (consoles and encourages) us in every trouble (calamity

and affliction), so that we may also be able to comfort (console and encourage) those who are in any kind of trouble or distress with the comfort (consolation and encouragement) with which we ourselves and comforted (consoled and encouraged) by God. Amp.

"Blessed are they that mourn: for they shall be comforted." "By these words Christ does not teach that mourning in itself has power to remove the guilt of sin. He gives no sanction to pretense or to voluntary humility. The mourning of which He speaks does not consist in melancholy and lamentation. While we sorrow on account of sin, we are to rejoice in the precious privilege of being children of God.

"We often sorrow because our evil deeds bring unpleasant consequences to ourselves; but this is not repentance. Real sorrow is the result of the working of the Holy Spirit. The Spirit reveals the ingratitude of the heart that has slighted and grieved the Saviour and brings us in contrition to the foot of the cross. By every sin Jesus is wounded afresh; and as we look upon Him whom we have pierced, we mourn for the sins that have brought anguish upon Him. Such mourning will lead to the renunciation of sin.

"The worldly may pronounce this sorrow a weakness; but it is the strength which binds the penitent to the Infinite One with links that cannot be broken. It shows that the angels of God are bringing to the soul graces that were lost through hardness of heart and transgression. The tears of the penitent are only the raindrops that precede the sunshine of holiness. This sorrow heralds a joy which will be a living fountain in the soul.

"Only acknowledge thine iniquity, that thou hast transgressed against the Lord thy God," "and I will not cause Mine anger to fall upon you; for I am merciful, said the Lord." Jer. 3:13, 12. "Unto them that mourn in Zion," He has appointed to give "beauty for ashes, the oil of joy for mourning, the garment of praise for the spirit of heaviness." Isa. 61:3

And for those who mourn in trial and sorrow there is comfort. The bitterness of grief and humiliation is better than the indulgences of sin. Through affiliation God reveals to us the plague spots in our characters, that by His grace we may overcome our faults. Unknown chapters in regards to ourselves are open to us, and the test comes, whether we will accept the reproof and the counsel of God. When brought into trial, we are not to fret and complain. We should not rebel, or worry ourselves out of the hand of Christ. We are to humble the soul before God. The ways of the Lord are obscure to him who desires to see things in a light pleasing to himself. They appear dark and joyless to our human nature. But God's ways are ways of mercy and the end is salvation. Elijah knew not what he was doing when in the desert he said that he had had enough of life, and prayed that he might die. The Lord in His mercy did not take him at his word. There was yet a great work for Elijah to do; and when his work was done, he was not to perish in discouragement and solitude in the wilderness. Not for him the descent into the dust of death, but the ascent into glory, with the convoy of celestial chariots to the throne on high.

God's word for the sorrowing is, "I have seen his ways, and will heal him: I will lead him also, and restore comforts unto him and to his mourners." I will turn their mourning into joy, and will comfort them, and make them rejoice from their sorrow." Isa. 57:18; Jer. 31:3. Ellen G. White—The Desire of Ages, p. 300-301

In preparing his disciples for His departure, Jesus said to them:

> And I will ask the Father, and He will give you another Comforter (Counselor, Helper, Intercessor, Advocate, Strengthener, and Standby), that He may remain with you forever—The Spirit of Truth, Whom the World cannot receive (welcome, take to its heart), because it does not see Him or know and recognize Him. But you know and recognize Him, for He lives with you [constantly] and will be in you. John 14:16, 17

There are two points in this passage that gets me excited. 1) The Comforter, who is the Holy Spirit will remain when he comes. 2) The Holy Spirit comes to dwell in the heart of the believer.

To all those who mourn the promise has been given—they shall be comforted. John 16:8 tells us that the Holy Spirit even has a work to do for the unregenerate.

> And when He comes, He will convict and convince the world and bring demonstration to it about sin and about righteousness (uprightness of heart and right standing with God) and about judgment.

"There are often incredible things in the lives of Christians, inexplicable except on the basis of a lack of a real sense of the sin involved. Strife for foremost position, envy, malice, evil thinking, impure acts, and hatred of one another—these exist principally because of an appalling lack of the sense of sin." The Coming of the Comforter, p. 70

The coming of the Spirit makes two things clear to the believer—

1. The holiness of God
2. The loathsomeness of sin

"Without the divine working man could do no good thing. God calls every man to repentance, yet man cannot even repent unless the Holy Spirit works upon his heart. Testimonies For The Church vol. 8 p. 64

"None are so vile, none have fallen so low, as to be beyond the working of this power. In all who will submit themselves to the Holy Spirit, a new principle of life is to be implanted; the lost image of God is to be restored in humanity."

"But man can not transform himself by the exercise of his will. He possesses no power by which this change can be effected. The leaven—something wholly from without—must be put into meal before the desired change can be wrought in it. So the grace of God must be received by the sinner before he can be fitted for the Kingdom of Glory. All the culture and education which the world can give, will fail of making a degraded child of sin a child of heaven. The renewing energy must come from God. The change can be made only by the Holy Spirit. All who would be saved, high or low, rich or poor, must submit to the working of this power." Christ Object Lessons, p. 96-97.

It is through the working of the Holy Spirit that the one who has been regenerated is brought into the experience of conversion. This conversion is the natural outgrowth of regeneration in the lives of all those who have been called unto God through Jesus Christ.

A study of the Old Testament will show that the two primary words for conversion are "Nacham" and "Shulah."

1. Nachum is used "to express a deep feeling of sorrow (niphal) or of relief (piel). In niphal—means to repent, and this repentance is often accompanied with a change of plan and of action, which is piel—it signifies to comfort or to comfort oneself."

2. Shubh—"Which is the most common word for conversion and means to turn, to turn about, and to return. This meaning is most prominent to the prophets, where it refers to Israel's return to the Lord, after it has departed from him. The word clearly shows that what the Old Testament calls conversion, is a return to Him from whom sin has separated man. This is a very import element in conversion." Louis Berkhof, "Systematic Theology, p. 480."

Turning to the New Testatment, the most common word for conversion is "Metanoia." This word has a connection to the verb "ginosko" to know, and applies to the consciousness of man. This word, "Metanoia" is translated repentance in our English Bible translations, to which Berkhof states, "this redering hardly does justice to the original, since it gives undue prominence to the emotional element. Ibid, p. 480. Trench points out that in the classics the word means:

1. To know after, after-knowledge;
2. To change the mind as the result of this after-knowledge;
3. Inconsequence of this change of mind, to regret the course pursued; and
4. A change of conduct for the future. Berkhof, p. 480-481

The principal idea in "Metanoia" is on having a general change of mind. This change is necessary because the Bible plainly states that both the mind and the conscience are defiled.

Titus 1:15 states:

> To the pure [in heart and conscience] all things are pure, but to the defiled and corrupt and unbelieving nothing is pure; their very minds and conscience are defiled and polluted. Amp.

Now, when a person is changed, he receives new knowledge and a new direction for his life. He will experience intellectual change—a better knowledge of God and His truth, and the acceptance of it.

2 Timothy 2:25 says:

> He must correct his opponents with courtesy and gentleness, in the hope that God may grant that they will repent and come. To know the truth [that they will perceive and recognize and become accurately acquainted with and acknowledge it].

This change leads to the act of making a conscious choice or decision to turn from self to God:

> So repent of this depravity and wickedness of years and pray to the Lord that, if possible, this contriving thought and purpose of your heart may be removed and disregarded and forgiven you. Acts 8:22 Amp.

Godly sorrow accompanies the change:

> For godly grief and the pain God is permitted to direct, produce a repentance that leads and contributes to salvation and deliverance from evil, and it never brings regret; but worldly grief (the hopeless sorrow that is characteristic of the pagan world) is deadly [breeding and ending in death]. 2 Corinthians 7:10

It should be noted here that "Metanoia" denotes a conscious opposition to the former condition of life. "To be converted, is not merely to pass from the conscious direction to another, but to do it with a clearly perceived aversion to the former direction . . . The converted person becomes conscious of his ignorance and error, his willfulness and folly. His conversion includes both faith and repentance." Systematic Theology p. 481

Another New Testament word for conversion is "Epistrophe" which imply that the turning spoken of is more specifically a returning. It stresses that a new relationship has been established, and that the life is now moving in another direction. Note the following:

> So repent (change your mind and purpose); turn around and return [to God], that your sins may be erased (blotted out, wiped clean), that times of

refreshing (of recovering from the effects of heat, of reviving with fresh air) may come from the presence of the Lord. Acts 3:19 Amp.

COUNSEL TO BROTHER P.

The following counsel was written in the late 1800's to a fellow Christian. It is taken from the book "Testimony for the Church, Vol. 2." Here we find the admonitions given to him.

Dear Brother P: While at—one year ago, we labored for your interest. I had been shown your dangers, and we were desirous of saving you; but we see you have not had strength to carry out the resolutions there made. I am troubled over the matter, and fear that I was not as faithful as I should have been in bringing before you all I knew of your case. Some things I withheld from you. While in Battle Creek in June, I was again shown that you were not making any advance, and that the reason you were not is that you have not made a clean track behind you. You do not enjoy religion. You have departed from God and righteousness. You have been seeking happiness in the wrong way, in forbidden pleasures; and you have no moral courage to forsake your sins that you may find mercy.

You did not view sin as heinous in the sight of God, and put it away; you failed to make thorough work; and when the enemy came in with his temptations, you did not resist him. Had you seen how offensive sin was in the sight of God, you would not so readily yielded to temptation. You were not so thoroughly converted as to abhor your life of sin and folly. Sin yet seemed pleasant to you, and you were loathe to yield up its delusive pleasures. Your innermost soul was not converted, and you soon lost that which you had gained.

Personal vanity in your case, as well as in that of many other has been a special hindrance to you. This has been a snare to you. Your professional friends have shown a special pleasure in your society, and this has gratified you. Weak-minded, sympathetic women have praised you and appeared charmed with your society; and you have felt a fascinating power upon you in their company. You did not realize, while spending in pleasure seeking these hours which belonged to your family, that Satan was weaving his net about your feet.

Satan has temptations laid for every step of your life. You have not been as economical of means as you should have been. You hate stinginess. This is all right; but you go to the opposite extreme, and your course has been marked with prodigality. Christ taught His disciples a lesson in feeding the five thousand. He wrought a great miracle and feed that vast multitude with five loaves and two small fishes. After all had been satisfied, He did not then regard the fragments indifferently, as if it were beneath His dignity to notice them. He who had power to work so notable a miracle, and to give food to so large a company, said to His disciples: "Gather up the fragments that remain, that nothing be lost." This is a lesson to us all, and one which we should not disregard.

You have a great work before you, and you cannot afford to waste another moment without taking hold of it. Brother P, I am alarmed for you; but I know that God loves you still, although your course has been wayward. If He did not have a special love for you He would not present your dangers before me a He has. You have engaged in jesting and sporting with men and women who have not the fear of God before them. Weak-headed and unprincipled women have retained you in their presence, and you were like a charmed bird. You seemed fascinated by these superficial persons. Angels of God were upon your track and have faithfully recorded every wrong act, every instance of departure from virtue's path.

Yes, every act, however secret you may have thought you were in its committal, has been opened to God, to Christ, and to the holy angels. A book is written of all the doings of the children of men. Not an item of this record can be concealed. There is only one provision made for the transgressor. Faithful repentance and confession of sin, and faith in the cleansing blood of Christ, will bring forgiveness, and pardon will be written against his name.

O my brother, had you made thorough work one year ago, the past precious year need not have been to you worse than a blank. You knew your Master's will, but did it not. You are in a perilous condition. Your sensibilities have been blunted to spiritual things; you have a violated conscience. Your influence is not to gather, but to scatter. You have no special interest in religious exercises. You are not a happy man. Your wife would write her interest with the people of God if you would get out of her way. She needs your help. Will you take hold of this work together?

Last June, I saw that your only hope of breaking the chain of your bondage was a removal from your associates. You had yielded to Satan's temptation until you were a weak man. You were a lover of pleasure more than a lover of God, and were fast traveling the downward path. I have been disappointed that you have continued in the same indifferent state in which you have been for years. You have known and experienced the love of God; and it has been your delight to do His will. You have delighted in the study of the word of God. You have been punctual at the prayer meetings. Your testimony has been from a heart which felt the quickening influences of the love of Christ. But you have lost your first love.

God now calls upon you to repent, to be zealous in the work. Your eternal happiness will be determined by the course you now pursue. Can you reject the invitation of mercy now offered? Can you choose your own way? Will you cherish pride and vanity, and lose your soul at last? The word of God plainly tells us that few will be saved, and that the greater number of them, even, who are called will prove themselves unworthy of everlasting life. They will have no part in heaven, but will have their portion with Satan, and experience the second of death.

Men and women may escape this doom if they will. It is true that Satan is the great originator of sin; yet, this does not excuse any man for sinning; for he cannot force men to do evil. He tempts them to it, and makes sin look enticing and pleasant; but he has to leave it to their own will whether they will do it or not. He does not force men to become intoxicated, neither does he force them to remain away from religious meetings; but he presents temptations in a manner to allure to evil, and man is a free moral agent to accept or refuse.

Conversion is a work that most do not appreciate. It is not a small matter to transform an earthly, sin-loving mind and bring it to understand the unspeakable love of Christ, the charms of His grace, and the Excellency of God, so that the soul shall be imbued with divine love and captivated with the heavenly mysteries. When he understands these things, his former life appears disgusting and hateful. He hates sin, and breaking his heart before God, he embraces Christ as the life and joy of the soul. He renounces his former pleasures. He has a new mind, new affections, new interest, new will; his sorrow's, and desires, and love are all new. The lust of the flesh, the lust of the eye and the pride of life, which have heretofore been preferred before Christ, are now turned from, and Christ is the charm of his life, the crown of his rejoicing. Heaven, which once possessed no charms, is now viewed in its riches and glory; and he contemplates it as his future home, where he shall see, love, and praise the One who hath redeemed him by His precious blood.

The work of holiness, which appeared wearisome, is now his delight. The word of God, which was dull and uninteresting, is now chosen as his study, the man of his counsel. It is as a letter written to him from God, bearing the inscription of the Eternal. His thoughts, his words, and his deeds are brought to this rule and tested. He trembles at the commands and threatening which it contains, while he firmly grasps its promises and strengthens his soul by appropriating them himself. The society of the most godly is now chosen by him, and the wicked, whose company he once loved, he no longer delights in. He weeps over those sins in them at which he once laughed. Self-love and vanity are renounced, and he lives unto God and is rich in good works. This is the sanctification which God requires. Nothing short of this will He accept.

I beg you, my brother, to search your heart diligently and inquire: "What road am I traveling, and where will it end?" You have reason to rejoice that your life has not been cut off while you have no certain hope of eternal life. God forbid that you should no longer neglect this work, and so perish in your sins. Do not flatter your soul with false hopes. You see no way to get hold again but one so humble that you cannot consent to accept it. Christ presents to you, even to you, my erring brother, a message of mercy: "Come; for all things are now ready." God is ready to accept you and to pardon all your transgressions, if you will but come. Though you have been a prodigal, and have separated from God and stayed away from Him so long, He will meet you even now. Yes; the Majesty of heaven invites you to come to Him, that you may have life. Christ is ready to cleanse your from sin when you lay hold upon Him. What profit have you found in serving sin? What profit in serving the flesh and the devil? Is it not poor wages you receive? Oh, turn ye, turn ye; for why will ye die?

You have had many convictions, many pangs of conscience. You have had so many purposes and made so many promises, and yet you linger and will not come to Christ that you may have life. Oh, that your heart may be impressed with a sense of this time, that you may now turn and live! Cannot you hear the voice of the true Shepherd in this message? How can you disobey? Trifle not with God, lest He leave you to your own crooked ways. It is life or death with you. Which will you choose? It is a fearful thing to contend with God and resist His pleadings. You may have the love of God burning upon the altar of your heart as you once felt it. You may commune with God as you have done in times past. If you will make a clean track behind you, you may again experience the riches of His grace, and your countenance again express His love.

It is not required of you to confess to those who know not your sin and errors. It is not your duty to publish a confession which will lead unbelievers to triumph; but to those to whom it is proper, who will take no advantage of your wrong, confess according to the word of God, and let them pray for you, and God will accept your work, and will heal you. For your soul's sake, be entreated to make thorough work for eternity. Lay aside your pride, your vanity, and make straight work. Come back again to the fold. The Shepherd's waiting to receive you. Repent, and do your first works, and again come into favor with God. Ellen G. White, "Testimonies for The Church, Vol. 2," p. 291-296.

True Conversion is born of godly sorrow that is according to God in the way prescribed by and acceptable to Him. This sorrow is not the kind that comes when one's wicked ways are being discovered or that kind that accompanies one's anticipation of being punished. We are talking here about genuine sorrow for sin, repentance of that sin, separation from the sin and determination from this point on to resist sin in all its forms by the grace of Jesus Christ.

In "godly sorrow" one must recognize and acknowledge that he has wronged God and his fellow men and must seek to do all in his power to right the wrong. He then orders his life to avoid making the same mistakes. This can be accomplish only be virtue of the grace of Christ which the Holy Spirit makes active in his life. True sorrow for sin involves the recognition of your accountability to God for your conduct, which is possible only when that relationship is acknowledged.

"Perhaps the supreme illustration of the difference between true and false sorrow for sin lies in the contrast between Peter and Judas during the trial of Jesus. Both felt bitter remorse, but with the one there was true sorrow for sin, which led to a new life in Christ; with the other there was only sorrow for the consequences, which led to utter despair and then suicide." SDA Bible Commentary vol. 6 p. 884

True conversion has two sides, and active aspect and a passive aspect. Both God and man are involved in the process. "Consequently, a twofold definition must be given of conversion: (a) Active conversion is that act of God whereby He causes the regenerated sinner, in His conscious life, to turn to Him in repentance and faith. (b) Passive conversion is the resulting conscious act of the regenerated sinner whereby he, through the grace of God, turns to God in repentance and faith. Berkhof, p. 483

It is important here to note some of the distinguishing attributes of conversion.

1. Conversion is the re-created act of God in which the condition of man is altered. Man becomes aware of the truth of his condition—worthy of condemnation, a fact that he acknowledges. Thus he is led to confidently trust in Jesus Christ by faith for his salvation. He accepts the blessed assurance that all his sins are forgiven on the basis of the merits of Christ.
2. Conversion has its beginnings in regeneration. Therefore, any conversion that does not have its roots in regeneration is false conversion.
3. Conversion involves the turning away from the old man of sin (with all his sin) and a putting on of the new man, a pressing toward holiness of life. The holy principles of the new life are now activated and the life is re-turned to a God-ward direction. This life is now lived in devotion and communion with God.
4. Conversion is a momentary change not a prolonged process.

Finally, it is necessary to emphasize two points:

1. The author of conversion is God. In Psalm 85:4 the writer acknowledges God as the one who does the turning he prays: "Turn us, O God of our salvation." "Restore us, O God of our salvation." Ephraim prays in Jeremiah 31:8—"Turn thou me, and I shall be turned." "Bring me back, that I may be restored." "The new principle of life that is implanted in the regenerate man, does not issue into conscious action by its own inherent power, but only through the illuminating and crucifying influence of the Holy Spirit."

Jesus says:

> "No one is able to come to Me unless the Father who sent me attracts and draws him and gives him the desire to come to Me . . ." John 6:44 Amp
>
> [Not in your own strength] for it is God who is all the while effectually at work in you [energizing and creating in you the power and desire], both to will and to work for His good pleasure and satisfaction and delight. Phil. 2:13

2. Man cooperates with God in conversion. This activity on man's part is always the result of the work God has already done in man. Look again at Phil. 2:13 above. The activeness of man in conversion is absolutely necessary!

   Let the wicked forsake his ways and the unrighteous man his thoughts; and let him return to the Lord . . . Isaiah 55:7

   . . . Return now each one from his evil way; reform your [accustomed] ways and make your [individual] actions good and right. Jeremiah 18:11

   . . . Repent, and be baptized every one of you in the name of Jesus Christ for the remission of sins, and ye shall receive the gift of the Holy Ghost. Acts 2:38

God bestows in every man the gift of repentance—He works in man to do of His will. Man response to this act of God by accepting His gift and reaching out in faith to walk in newness of life by the grace of Christ. Repentance, therefore, is one of the components of conversion that we will now turn our attention too.

Repentance

In order to get an accurate understanding of this important word, we must give some consideration to the original Hebrew and Greek.

We will give attention to two Hebrew words:

1. "Naham"—originally it implies difficulty in breathing, hence "to pant," "to sigh," "to groan." It came to signify, "to lament" or "to grieve," and when the emotion was produced by the desire of good for others, it merged into compassion and sympathy, and when incited by a consideration of one's own character and deeds it means to "to rue," "to repent." (The Intl Standard Bible Encycl., Vol. 4, p. 2558) This word is primarily used in reference to God. It does not carry the idea of one's personal sin or a turning from an evil path. It fills the heart of the Holy God with grief over the sinful course of man. His emotion is awakened and in love He changes His course of dealing with man.

   And it repented the Lord that he had made man on the earth, and it grieved him at his heart. Gen. 6:6 KJV

   And the Lord regretted that He had made man on the earth, and He was grieved at heart. Gen. 6:6 Amp.

   "The 'repentance' of God is an expression referring to the pain of divine love occasioned by the sinfulness of man. It presents the truth that God, in consistency with His immutability, assumes a changed position in respect to changed man. The mention of divine grief at man's deprived state is a touching indication that God did not hate man. Human sin fills the divine heart with deep felt grief and pity. It excites all the fathomless ocean of sympathy for sinning man which infinite love is capable. Nonetheless, it moves Him also to judicial retribution." SDA Bible Commentary vol. 1 p. 251

2. Shubh—this word is used largely by the prophets, and it promotes the idea of a radical change in attitude toward sin and God. It

entails (a) a conscious separation fom sin, (b) a personal decision to abandon sin and (c) to come into a relationship with God. "Shubh" is used to show man's turning away from sin and turning into righteousness. It is also used to show the complete spiritual change that God only can bring, "turn us, O God of our salvation." Ps. 85:4 If God does not do the turning we will never be turned.

We will now turn to the Greek words to get the New Testament teaching on repentance.

1. Metamelomai—"to have a feeling or care, concern or regret," it also expresses the emotional aspect of repentance. This feeling may lead to genuine repentance or it may lead to just simply remorse. Let us view two examples:
    a. And he answered, I will not; but afterward he changed his mind and went. (Matt. 21:29)—Genuine repentance.
    b. When Judas, His betrayer, saw that [Jesus] was condemned, [Judas was afflicted in mind and troubled for his former folly; and] with remorse [with little more than a selfish dread of the consequences] he brought back the thirty pieces of silver to the chief priests and the elders. Matt. 27:3
    This repentance of Judas was only in the sense of remorse and regret. His repentance was not in the sense of the abandonment of his sin.

2. Metanoeo—"to have another mind," "to change the opinion or purpose with regard to sin." It indicates the spiritual change that is implied in the sinner's return to God.

3. Epistrepho—this work is "used to bring out more clearly the distinct change wrought in repentance." It is also used to show the spiritual change from sin to God.
    For they themselves volunteer testimony concerning us, telling what an entrance we had among you, and how you turned to God

from [your] idols to serve a God who is alive and true and genuine.
I Thess.1:19

It is used to strengthen faith;

And the presence of the Lord was with them with power, so
that a great number [learned] to believe (to adhere to and trust in
and rely on the Lord) and turned and surrendered themselves to
Him. Acts 11:21

Repentance has three elements which are called by some the
psychological elements.

1. The Intellectual Element

Repentance is that radical change that takes place in the mind
of the sinner which lends him to turn from his life of sin which
leads to death. This change affects the intellect, the emotions and
the will. The sinner must understand the sinfulness of sin and see
himself as coming short of the commandments of God.

For no person will be justified (made righteous, acquitted and
judged acceptable in His sight by observing the works prescribed
by the Law. For [the real function of] the Law is to make men
recognize and be conscious of the sin [not mere perception, but an
acquaintance with sin which works toward repentance, faith, and
holy character]. Rom. 3:20

2. The Emotional Element

There is a change of feeling in the sinner's heart which is
manifested in sorrow for the sin that has been committed against
God. Even though feeling and repentance are not equals, feeling
can be a powerful impulse to genuine repentance.

"There must be a consciousness of sin in its effect on man
and in its relation to God before there can be a hearty turning

away from unrighteousness. The feeling naturally accompanying repentance implies a conviction of personal sin and sinfulness and an earnest appeal to God to forgive according to His mercy." The Intl Standard Bible Encyclopedia Vol.4 p 2559

3. The Voluntary or Volitional Element

There is a change of the will, a change of the mind, and a change of purpose, for a sincere and complete turning to God involves an understanding of the true nature of sin, an inward turning away from sin and an attitude to seek forgiveness and cleansing.

"Repentance is only a condition of salvation and not its meritorious ground. The motives for repentance are chiefly found in the goodness of God, in Divine love, in the pleading desire to have sinners saved, in the inevitable consequences of sin, in the universal demands of the gospel, and in the hope of spiritual life and membership in the kingdom of heaven." Intl Standard Bible Encyclopedia Vol.4 p. 2559

God say to His people, "As I live, says the Lord God, I have no pleasure in the death of the wicked, but rather that the wicked turn from his way and live. Turn back, turn back, from your evil ways, for why will you die, O house of Israel?" Ezek. 33:11 And saying, "The [appointed period of] time is fulfilled (completed), and the Kingdom of God is at hand; repent (have a change of mind which issues in regret for past sins and in change of conduct for the better) and believe (trust in, rely on, and adhere to) the good news (the Gospel)." Mk. 1:15 Amp.

Or are you [so blind as to] trifle with and presume upon and despise and underestimate the wealth His kindness and forbearance and long-suffering patience? Are you unmindful or actually ignorant [of the fact] that God's kindness is intended to lead you to repent [to change your mind and inner man to accept God's will]? Rom. 2:4

When we take into account what the scripture has to say concerning repentance, it is very clear that repentance is totally an inward act and is separate from the change of life that proceeds from it. Confession of sin and reparation (the act or process of making amends) of wrongs are fruits borne to repentance.

PSALM 51 is a Psalm of David that was written after he had sinned with Bathsheba. In it we find an example of true repentance:

"Have mercy upon me, O God, according to Your steadfast love, according to the multitude of Your tender mercy *and* loving-kindness blot out my transgressions.

Wash me thoroughly [and repeatedly] from my iniquity *and* guilt and cleanse me and make me wholly pure from sin!

For I am conscious of my transgressions and I acknowledge them; my sin is ever before me.

Against You, You only, have I sinned and done that which is evil in Your sight, so that You are justified in your sentence and faultless in Your judgment.

Behold, I was brought forth in [a state of] iniquity; my mother was sinful who conceived me [and I too am sinful].

Behold, You desire truth in the inner being; make me therefore to know wisdom in my inmost heart.

Purify me with hyssop, and I shall be clean [ceremonially]' wash me, and I shall [in reality] be whiter than snow.

Make me to hear joy and gladness and be satisfied let the bones which You have broken rejoice.

Hide Your face from my sins and blot out all my guilt and iniquities.

Create in me a clean heart, O God, and renew a right, persevering, and steadfast spirit within me.

Cast me not away from Your presence and take not Your Holy Spirit from me.

Restore to me the joy of Your salvation and uphold me with a willing spirit.

Then will I teach transgressors Your ways, and sinners will be converted and return to You.

Deliver me from bloodguiltiness *and* death, O God, the God of my salvation, *and* my tongue shall sing aloud of Your righteousness (Your rightness and Your justice).

O Lord, open my lips and my mouth shall bring forth Your praise.

For you delight not in sacrifice, or else would I give it; You find no pleasure in burnt offering.

My sacrifice (the sacrifice acceptable) to God is a broken spirit; a broken spirit and a contrite heart (broken down with sorrow for sin and humbly and thoroughly penitent, such O God, You will not despise.

Do good in Your good pleasure to Zion; rebuild the walls of Jerusalem.

Then will You delight in the sacrifices of righteousness, *justice* and right, with burnt offerings and whole burnt offerings; then bullocks will offered upon Your altar.

This prayer of David should be the petition of every child of God. As he prayed for forgiveness he besought God to renew the heart that he will walk in constant obedience. The consciousness of sin will leave us heartbroken before God. There will be no words of excuse, no attempt to justify, no battle wage against the justice of God's law that condemns. The cold, hard heart will be melted. In meekness each will take the responsibility for his own sin. Such experience will awake humility in the heart of the children of God. Contreary to the world view, humility is strength, for it was the world redeemer who said—"Blessed are the meek for they shall inherit the earth." Matthew 5:5

CHAPTER FOUR

MASTER SELF-CONTROL

Key 3

Living a meek and quiet life.

The highest evidence of nobility in a Christian is self-control. If we emulate the humility of Christ, we will surmount above the slights, the annoyances, the trespasses, to which we are daily exposed. They shall not be allowed to cast a gloom over our spirit. The Christian strength that gives victory in Christ is their lowliness of heart. This reveals their connection with heaven.

A study of the Beatitudes will reveal a progression of Christian growth, development and experience. Those who have felt and acknowledge their need of Christ, who mourn; because of their rebellion and who sit and learn with Christ in the school of affliction, will learn meekness from their divine Teacher.

It was not a common thing for men to have the characteristics of patience and gentleness. Moses under the guidance of the Holy Spirit was such that he was made the meekest man upon the earth. This statement was not regarded by the people as a commendation, but rather one that was meted with pity or contempt. Jesus, however, places meekness among the first qualifications of His Kingdom. We can in His life and character see the revelation of this divine, precious grace.

Jesus is the ultimate example of humility:

> Who, although being essentially one with God and in the form of God [possessing the fullness of the attributes which make God God], did not think this equality with God was a thing to be eagerly grasped or retained.
>
> But stripped Himself [of all privileges and rightful dignity], so as to assume the guise of a servant (slave), in that He became like men and was born a human being. Phil. 2:6,7 Amp.
>
> Jesus walked among men, not as a King, to demand worship but as a man with a mission to be of service to others. He was the redeemer of the world, greater in might, strength, glory and power than was the host of heavenly angels. Yet, we find united in His being meekness and humility that attracted all to Him.

Christ possessed all the eternal qualities and characteristics of God. He was one with the Father, and stood far above every other power. Conscious of His equality with God, Christ decided to give up the glory associated with His exalted state in order to accomplish His purpose of saving lost humanity. Can our human mind fully understand the depth of Christ's voluntary humiliation?

Christ literally emptied Himself. He said, I lay it down voluntarily. [I put it from Myself] I am authorized and have power to lay it down (to resign it) and I am authorized and have power to take it back again. John 10:18 "It was not possible for Christ to retain all the tokens of divinity and still accomplish the incarnation." SDA Bible Commentary vol. 7 p. 155

Paul is showing that Christ emptied Himself and took up the essential attributes of a slave. The outstanding characteristic of a slave is to render unquestioned obedience to the master. In the same way, as a slave, the Son undertook to render obedience to the Father. The passion of His life was not divine sovereignty but to render service. His life was subordinated to the will of His Father and thus became the outworking of the will of God.

> "But the Son of God was surrendered to the Father's will and dependent upon His power. So utterly was Christ emptied of self that He made no plans for Himself. He accepted God's plans for Him, and day by day the Father unfolded His plans. So should we depend upon God, that our lives may be the simple outworking of His will." Desire of Ages

How can all of this happen? Certainly the human mind cannot comprehend it all, for herein lies part of the great mystery of godliness. By looking unto Christ we should understand how all our sacrifices are nothing by way of comparison with the sacrifice He made of Himself. Must we be so lifted up with self that we find it difficult or impossible to yield our wills to the will of the Father? When we develop the true spirit of Christ, when He is dwelling within us we will live the life of the Son of God by following His example of humility.

> "Our belief in the deity of Christ must not weaken in any way our belief in His complete manhood. If Christ was not absolutely a man, if His divinity in the

least degree qualified His humanity, then He practically ceased to be an example, and, indeed, a substitute." SDA Bible Commentary vol. 7 p. 155

Christ counsels His followers to:

> "Take my yoke upon you and learn of Me, for I am gentle (meek) and humble (lowly) in heart, and you will find rest (relief and ease, refreshment and recreation, and blessed and quiet) for your souls. Matt.11:29 Amp.

Originally a yoke was used as an instrument of service; it was created to make cooperative effort possible. It became a sign of submission in time of war to the conqueror. "A victorious general mounted a yoke on two spears and made the defeated army march under it in token of submission." The yoke as it came to be used on animals; was to make the burden lighter and easier to bear.

In the Christian sense, taking the yoke of Christ means to adopt His way of life. The Christian is called to submit to the discipline and training of Christ's way of life. His yoke is His divine will summed up in the law of God.

"Take My yoke upon you," Jesus says. The yoke is an instrument of service. Cattle are yoked for labor, and the yoke is essential that they may labor effectually. By this illustration Christ teaches us that we are called to service so long as life shall last. We are to take upon us His yoke, that we may be co-workers with Him.

The yoke that binds to service is the law of God. The great law of love revealed in Eden, proclaimed upon Sinai, and in the new covenant written in the heart, is that which binds the human worker to the will of God. If we were left to follow our own inclinations, to go just where our will would lead us, we should fall into Satan's ranks and become possessors of his attributes. Therefore God confines us to His will, which is high, and noble, and elevating. He desires that we shall patiently and wisely take up the duties of service. The yoke of service Christ Himself has borne in humanity. He said, "I delight to do Thy will, O My God: yea, Thy law is within My heart." Ps. 40:8 "I came down from Heaven, not to do Mine own will, but the will of Him that sent Me." John 6:38 Love for God, zeal for His glory, and love for fallen humanity, brought Jesus to earth to suffer and to die. This was the controlling power of His life. The principle He bids us adopt." Desire of Ages p. 329-330

He says in Matthew 16: 24

> If anyone desires to be My disciples, let him deny himself [disrespect, lose sight of, and forget himself, and his own interests] and take up his cross and follow Me [cleave steadfastly to Me, conform wholly to My example in living and, if need be, in dying also] Amp.

Jesus here addressed all the disciples, not only the twelve but all those who desire to follow Him. In order to be His disciple one must renounce himself, submit his will to Christ and henceforth live for Christ rather than for himself. He must further take upon himself the responsibilities that go along with discipleship even if it calls for him to lay down his life.

One who was condemned to die by crucifixion literally had to take up his cross and carried it to the place of execution. It seems that Christ was not linking cross bearing to the little difficulties and obstacles that the disciple will face from day to day but rather to the need of being ready to face death itself. In Luke 9:23 Christ present the thought that the disciple must take up his cross daily. In this He points to the life of service to which the disciple is called.

All who would contemplate discipleship must first renounce themselves, their own plans, their own desires, they must be prepared to bear any cross that responsibilities call them to take up, and they must follow in the footsteps of Jesus. To follow Jesus is to pattern our lives after his life, and to serve God and our fellow men as He did.

When in vision, Daniel saw one like the son of man, and was driven to say, "there remained no strength in me: for my comeliness was turned in me into corruption, and I retained no strength. (Daniel 10:8) The same will be the experience of those who behold Christ in His self-denial and lowliness of heart.

> Human nature is ever struggling for expression, ready for contest: but he who learns of Christ is emptied of self, of pride of love, of supremacy, and there is silence in the soul. Self is yielded to the disposal of the Holy Spirit. Then we are not anxious to have the highest place. We have no ambition to crowd and elbow ourselves into notice; but we feel that our highest place is at the feet of our Savior. We look to Jesus, waiting for His hand to lead, listening for His voice to guide. "E.G. White—Thought from the Mount of Blessing, p. 16"

The apostle Paul had this to say of his own experience:

> I have been crucified with Christ [in Him I have shared His crucifixion]; it is no longer I who live, but Christ (the Messiah) lives in me; and the life I now live in the body I live by faith in (by adherence to and reliance on and complete trust in) the Son of God, who loved me and gave Himself up for me. Gal. 2:29

When Christ is received in the heart as an abiding guest, the peace of God which passes all understanding, will keep our hearts and minds through Christ Jesus. Even thought our Savior lived in the midst of conflict, His life was a life of peace. He was constantly being pursued by His enemies yet, He said, "he who sent Me is ever with Me; My Father has not left Me alone, for I always do what pleases Him. John 8:29 No storm of human or Satanic wrath was able to disturb the calm of His perfect communion with God—His Father.

He is now saying to us:

> Peace I leave with you; My [own] peace I now give and bequeath to you. Not as the world give do I give to you. Do not let your hearts be troubled, neither let them be afraid. [Stop allowing yourself to be agitated and disturbed; and do not permit yourselves to be fearful and intimidated and cowardly and unsettled.] John 14:27

Our peace is destroyed by love of self. When self is alive, we are fully prepared to guard it from death and insult. When, on the other hand we are dead, and our life is hid with Christ in God, we will not take to heart neglect and slight. We shall become deaf to reproach and blind to scorn and insult.

Love endures long and is patient and kind; love never is envious nor boils over with jealousy, is not boastful, vain or glorious, does not display itself haughtily. It is not conceited (arrogant and inflated with pride); it is not rude (unmannerly) and does not act unbecomingly. Love (God's love in us) does not insist on its own rights or its own way, for it is not self-seeking; it is not touchy or fretful or resentful; it takes no account of the evil done to it [it pays no attention to a suffered wrong]. It does not rejoice at injustice and unrighteousness, but rejoices when right and truth prevail. Love bears up under anything and everything that comes, is ever ready to believe the best of every person, its hopes are fadeless under all circumstances, and it endures everything [without weakening]. Love never fails [never fades out or becomes obsolete or comes to an end]. I Cor. 13:4-8 Amp.

Happiness derived from earthly sources is unstable and subject to changeable circumstances. The peace that comes from Christ, however, is a constant and abiding peace. This peace depends not on any circumstances in life. Christ is the fountain of living water, and happiness drawn from Him can never fail.

"The meekness of Christ, manifested in the home, will make the inmates happy; it provokes no quarrel, gives back no angry answer, but soothes the irritated temper and diffuses a gentleness that is felt by all within its charmed circle. Wherever cherished, it makes the families of the earth a part of the one great family above." C.D.L. p.16-17

To the listening multitude Jesus said, "blessed are the meek." The word meek comes for the Greek word "praeis," its primary meaning is mild, gentle. It indicates kindness, humility, self-centered, disciplined or controlled spirit. In the Old Testament, meekness is from the world "anaw"—suffering, oppressed, afflicted, denoting the spirit produced under such experiences. It is generally associated with some form of oppression. The meek are the special object of divine regard.

Marvin Vincent, writing about meekness says, "the Christian word, describes an inward quality, and that as related primarily to God. The equanimity, mildness, kindness, represented by the classical word, are found in self-control or in natural disposition. The Christian meekness is based on humility, which is not a natural quality but an outgrowth of a renewed nature. To the pagan the word often implied condescension, to the Christian it implies submission." He continues by saying that "the meekness of the Christian springs from a sense of the inferiority of the creature to the creator and especially of the sinful creature to the Holy God." Vincent's Word Studies in the N. T. Vol. p. 37

Who are the meek?

1. The meek is controlled and disciplined. The body, mind, passion, urges, behaviors, speech, touch and sight are always under control.

The avenues of the soul—the five senses—are so guarded that nothing that can defile is allowed to enter.

Rom. 6:12 states,

> "Let not sin therefore rule as King in your mortal (short-lived, perishable) bodies, to make you yield to its cravings and be subject to its lusts and evil passions." Amp.

The meek will not allow sin to continue reigning in his life as it did in the past. As a believer he died with Christ so that sin may no longer have any authority over him. Even though the old man is crucified with Christ, we remained with a mortal body. We are still faced with earthly desires and cravings. Sin remains a powerful force. If we so choose, sin may still have control over us. Even when we are born again of the Holy Spirit the earthly desires of the flesh are very much alive. Being born again, however, places us in harmony with higher power by which we can exterminate the powers of sin. It is still up to every individual to determine whether we will give our allegiance to sin or to Christ.

> "Our experience of yesterday is not sufficient for today. Though we may have dies to sin yesterday, our "old man" may rear his ugly head again today. Only by keeping our old selves continually and completely dead to sin, as represented by our baptism, are we able to live daily unto God. And this experience is possible only through union with Jesus Christ, by a faith in Him that is so real and so constant that like Him we hate sin and love righteousness." SDA Bible Commentary vol. 6 p. 540

James 3:2 says,

> "For we all often stumble and fall and offend in many things. And if anyone does not offend in speech [never say the wrong things], he is a fully developed character and a perfect man, able to control his whole body and to curb his entire nature. Amp.

2. The meek is humble, not prideful

    a. Humility toward God—the meek accepts God dealings without complaint or resistance as absolutely wise and good. He acknowledges his need for God's hand upon every aspect of his life.
    b. Humility toward men—the meek accepts opposition, insult, provocation and injuries with the belief that God will vindicate. He accepts that he is not the perfect example of mankind, nor is he the summit of education among men. He does not claim to have it all or know it all. He is humble.

3. The meek is gentle, he is not easily provoked. In his relation with others he is always in control of his emotion. He is cool, even tempered to give a soft answer.

    Barnes says that "meekness produces peace. It is proof of true greatness of soul." He says further "it comes from a heart too great to be moved by little insults. It looks upon those who offend them with pity. He that is constantly ruffled; that suffers every little insult of injury to throw him off his guard and to raise a storm of passions within, is at the mercy of every mortal that chooses to disturb him. He is like the troubled sea that cannot rest, whose waters cast up mire and dirt." Albert Barns Notes—p. 44

Look at this counsel given to us by the word of God:

2 Timothy 2:24

> And the servant of the Lord must not be quarrelsome (fighting and contending). Instead, he must be kindly to everyone and mild-tempered [preserving the bond of peace]; he must be a skilled and suitable teacher, patient and forbearing and willing to suffer wrong. Amp. Bible

I Cor. 13:5

> It is not conceited (arrogant and inflated with pride); it is not rude (unmannerly) and does not act unbecomingly. Love (God's love in us) does not insist on its own rights or its own way, for it is not self-seeking; it is not touchy or fretful or resentful; it takes no account of the evil done to it [it pays no attention to a suffered wrong].

4. The meek is forgiving, never revengeful. Matt. 6:14

> For if you forgive people their trespasses [their reckless and willful sins, leaving them, letting them go, and giving up resentment], your heavenly Father will also forgive you.

Rom. 12:19

> Beloved, never avenge yourselves, but leave the way open for [God's] wrath; for it is written, Vengeance is Mine, I will repay (requite), says the Lord.

5. The meek is quiet

Psalms 4:4

> Be angry [or stand in awe] and sin not; commune
> with your own hearts upon your beds and be silent
> (sorry for the things you say in your hearts). Selah
> [pause, and calming think of that]!

> (a) The meek surrenders quietly to God recognizing his
>   great need and goes before God depending daily for
>   guidance and care.
>   Let be and be still, and know (recognizing and
>   understand) that I am God. I will be exalted among
>   the nations! I will be exalted in the earth! Ps. 46:10
> (B) The meek walks quietly before men, he is controlled in
>   all thing—both in his speech and his behavior.

I Thessalonians 4:11

> To make it your ambition and definitely endeavor
> to live quietly and peacefully, to mind your own affairs,
> and to work with your hands, as we charged you.

The KJV puts it this way—"And that ye study to be quiet, and
to do your own business, and to work with your own hands, as we
commanded you." The Thessalonians where counsel by Paul to be
ambitious, to aspire, to live a quiet and calm life. He calls on them to
labor and "mind your own affairs." It is clear that some were meddling
in the affairs of others, being busybodies. These are those who are busy
doing things that are unimportant, things that do not concern them,
and are involved in everybody's business but their own. The medicine
for such a condition is honest work. For those who are committed to

their own task will not find the time or have the desire to be meddling in the business of others. Busybodiness as a business produces tattling, evil-speaking, gossiping and the like.

Read the following carefully:

> Difficulties are often caused by the vendors of gossip, whose whispered hints and suggestions poison unsuspecting minds and separate the closest friends. Mischief-makers are seconded in their evil work by the many who stand with open ears and evil heart, saying: "Report . . . . And we will report it." This sin should not be tolerated among the followers of Christ. No Christian parent should permit gossip to be repeated in the family circle or remarks to be made disparaging the members of the church. Testimonies For The Church vol. 5 p. 242-242

The counsel of Paul to the Thessalonians and to the Christian church in this age can be summed up in this—the children of God should aim to be independent and not depend on others for their support.

I Peter 3:4

> But let it be the inward adorning and beauty of the hidden person of the heart, with the incorruptible and unfading charm of a gentle and peaceful spirit, which [is not anxious or wrought up, but] is very precious in the spirit of God.

The true self is not what can be seen on the outside but what is hidden from the sight—the inward person. The time spent in beautifying the character—the heart—with Christ-like traits is much more beneficial than the time dedicated to the outward decoration of the body.

The ornamentation that God desires His people to have is the robe of righteousness that Christ has promised to clothe all who accept Him by faith and come to him for leadership. This will speak well of our religion and our God to unbelieving friends and relatives. The inconspicuous simplicity of the Christian woman will sharply contrast the brazenness of those who call attention to themselves with "eye-catching hair styles, glittering ornaments and up-to-the minute clothing.

The Christian peace of mind is not reliant on changing fashionable styles but on Christ who is "the same yesterday, and today and forever" (Heb. 13:8). Indeed fellowship with Christ is worth far more than that of vacillating men. The value of golden ornaments and loaded apparel cannot stand in comparison with the perpetual value of men and women who are truly converted.

In meekness and quietness these godly women placed their hopes for acknowledgment and safekeeping in the promises of their God. All their desires were in agreement with God's sketch for their lives.

"The meek [Jesus says,] shall inherit the earth." It was through the desire for self-exaltation that sin entered our world. Our first parents lost their God-given authority over this earth—their kingdom. It was through self-abnegation that Christ redeemed that which was lost. Today we are called to overcome as He did.

Revelations 3:21 says:

> He who overcomes (is victorious), I will grant him to sit beside Me on My throne, as I Myself overcame (was victorious) and sat down beside My Father on His throne.

Through humility and self-surrender we may become heirs with Christ when the meek shall fully inherit the earth.

Psalms 37:10 states:

> But the meek [in the end] shall inherit the earth and shall delight themselves in the abundance of peace.
> The earth that is promised to the meek shall not be darkened with the shadow of death or curse.

2 Peter 3:13 says:

> But we look for new heavens and a new earth according to His promise, in which righteousness [uprightness, freedom from sin, and right standing with God) is to abide.

Revelations 22:3

> There shall no longer exist there anything that is accursed (detestable, foul, offensive, impure, hateful, or horrible). But the throne of God and of the Lamb shall be in it, and His servants shall worship Him [pay divine honors to Him and do His holy service].

Revelations 21:4

> God will wipe away every tear from their eyes; and death shall be no more, neither shall there be anguish (sorrow and mourning), nor grief nor pain any more, for the old condition and the former order of things have passed away.

This world will pass away, and conditions as we know them shall be no more. In the Kingdom that God shall establish, all things shall be made new. There will be nothing therein that will bear the mark of the curse of sin. In that land every tear shall be wiped away. "And the Lord God will wipe away tears from all faces; and the reproach of His people He will take away off all the earth." Isa. 25:8 "And the sound of weeping will no more be heard in it, nor the cry of distress." Isa. 65:19.

John points out that "the death"—the principle of death that entered our world as a result of sin—shall be no more. Praise the Lord that the death we know and fear shall be destroyed. The Apostle Paul says—"Death is swallowed up in victory." Literally he says, "The death was swallowed down in victory (I Cor. 15:54)." The last enemy that shall be destroyed is death—[the death] (I Cor. 15:54).

Grief, the type that goes together with bereavement shall be no more because all causes for sorrow will be absolutely eradicated. Crying shall not be known in that land for every cause for crying will be eliminated. The misery and anguish caused by pain shall be over, for pain will be completely taken away from the eternal home of the saved—the earth the meek shall inherit. The meek then, as he looks toward the fulfillment of this glorious promise will strive to learn more and more of his wonderful redeemer. In the words of Jesus he will "hunger and thirst after righteousness until he is filled." Matthew 5:6

CHAPTER FIVE

——————•———————

HUNGER AND THIRST AFTER RIGHTEOUSNESS

Key 4

Hunger and thirst after righteousness.

A sense of unworthiness will lead the heart to hunger and thirst for righteousness. Those who make room in their heart for Jesus shall experience His love. Those who long to bear the likeness of the character of the Son of God shall be satisfied.

The blessing is here given to those who experience hunger and thirst of the soul. "As the heart panteth after the water brooks, so panteth my soul after thee, O God. My soul thirsteth for God, for the living God. When shall I come and appear before God? (Ps. 42:1-2 KJV) Only those who yearn for righteousness with the enthusiasm of one starving for lack of food, or for want of water, will find it.

There is no earthly source that can satisfy the hungering and thirsting of the soul. Material riches, insightful philosophies, the contended physical appetites, honor and great power all fall miserably short of meeting the souls need. After King Solomon had experimented with all of these methods, he soberly concluded that "all is vanity." Therein he found no satisfaction or happiness for which the heart needs. He came to the wise conclusion that recognition and cooperation with his Creator will provide the only lasting satisfaction.

> All has been heard, the end of the matter is: Fear
> God [revere and worship Him, knowing that He is]
> and keep His commandments for this is the whole
> of man [the full, original purpose of his creation, the
> object of God's providence, the root of character, the
> foundation of all happiness, the adjustment to all
> inharmonious circumstances and conditions under
> the sun] and the whole [duty] for every man. Eccl.
> 12:13 Amp.

In another discourse recorded in John 6:26-59, Jesus discussed more fully the principles He set forth in the Sermon on the Mount. There Jesus presents Himself, as the bread for which all men should hunger. By partaking of this bread the spiritual life is sustained and the soul's hunger satisfied. Those who hunger and thirst are encouraged to come to Christ and receive food and drink "without money and without price." (Isa. 55:1, 2) Man has no desire in and of himself to yearn after the things of God. Thus, the longing of the soul for righteousness is confirmation that Christ has already started His work in the life.

To the Greeks righteousness consisted in obeying the rules of their customs. To the Jews it was conformity to the requirements of the law as construed by Jewish tradition. Paul in correcting Peter has this to say about righteousness—

Yet we know that a man is justified or reckoned righteous and in right standing with God not by works of the Law, but [only] through faith and [absolute] reliance on and adherence to and trust in Jesus Christ (the Messiah, the Anointed One). [Therefore] even we [ourselves] have believed on Christ Jesus, in order to be justified by faith in Christ and not by works of the Law [for we cannot be justified by any observance of the ritual of the Law given by Moses], because by keeping legal rituals and by works no human being can ever be justified (declared righteous and put in right standing with God). But if, in our desire and endeavor to be justified in Christ (to be declared righteous and put in right standing with God wholly and solely through Christ], we have shown ourselves sinners also and convicted of sin, does that make Christ a minister (a party and contributor) to our sin? Banish the thought! [Of course not!] For if I [or any other who have taught that the observance of the Law of Moses is not essential to being justified by God should now by word or practice teach or intimate that it is essential to] build up again what I tore down, I prove myself a transgressor. For I through the Law [under the operation of the curse of the Law] have [in Christ's death for me] myself died to the Law and all the Law's demand upon me, so that I may [henceforth] live to and for God. I have been crucified with Christ [in Him I have shared His crucifixion]: it is no longer I who live, but Christ (the Messiah) lives in me; and the life I now live in the body I live by faith in (by adherence to and reliance on and complete trust in) the Son of God, who loved me and gave Himself up for me. [Therefore, I do not treat God's gracious gift as something of minor importance and defeat its very purpose]: I do not set aside and invalidate and frustrate and nullify the grace (unmerited favor) of God. For if justification (righteousness, acquittal from guilt) comes, through [observing the ritual of] the Law, then Christ (the Messiah) died groundlessly and to no purpose and in vain. [His death was then wholly superfluous.] Gal. 2:16-21 Amp

Instead of going about trying to institute their own righteousness, Christians are counsel to submit "themselves unto the righteousness of

God" (Rom 10:3). The righteousness that is sought after is that which is through the faith of Christ—And that I may [actually] be found and known as in him, not having any [self-achieved] righteousness that can be called my own, based on my obedience to the Law's demands (ritualistic uprightness and supposed right standing with God thus acquired), but possessing that [genuine righteousness] which comes through faith in Christ (the Anointed One), the [truly] right standing with God, which comes from God by [saving] faith. (Phil. 3:9)

> "The righteousness of Christ is both imputed and imparted. Imputed righteousness brings justification. But the justified soul grows in grace. Through the power of the indwelling Christ he conforms his life to the requirements of the moral law as set forth by Jesus' own precept and example. This is imparted righteousness." Christ Object Lesson p. 310

This is what Christ was teaching when He instructed His listeners to be perfect as their Father in heaven is perfect. Paul points out that the perfect life of Jesus made it possible for the just condition of the law to be fulfilled in every Christian who walks not according to the flesh but according to the Spirit.

Righteousness is holiness, having the likeness of God, and God is love. Righteousness in the conformity to God's law, for Ps. 119:172 says, "all Thy commandments are righteousness." Paul makes it clear that "love is the fulfilling of the law." Rom. 3:10. There can be no righteousness without the act of love in obedience. Righteousness is love, and this love is the light and the life of God. The righteousness of God is, therefore, embodied in Christ Jesus. We receive righteousness by receiving Christ.

Righteousness is not and cannot be obtained by painful effort or tedious toil, not by sacrifices or gifts, it is a gift freely given to every soul who hungers and thirsts to receive it. "Wait and listen, everyone who is thirsty; come to the waters; and he who has no money; come buy and eat! Yes, come buy [priceless, spiritual] wine and milk without money and without price [simply for the self-surrendered that accepts the blessing"] Isa. 55:1 This is the righteousness or the vindication which they obtain from Me [this is that which I impart to them as their justification, said the Lord," and, "this is His name by which He shall be called: The Lord Our Righteousness." Isa. 54:17; Jer. 23:6

Jesus dispels the idea that man can supply that which will satisfy the hunger and thirst of the soul. He says,

> Behold, I stand at the door and knock; if anyone hears and listens to and heeds My voice and opens the door, I will come in to him and will eat with him, and he [will eat] with Me.
>
> I am the Bread of Life, He who comes to Me will never be hungry, and he who believes in cleaves to and trusts in and relies on Me will never thirst any more (at any time). Rev. 3:20; John 6:35

As food is needed to sustain physical strength, we need Christ, who is the Bread from heaven to sustain spiritual life and give strength to do the works of God. Just as the body is continually receiving the nourishment that prolongs life and vigor, in the same way the soul must be continuously communing with Christ. Surrendering to Him and depending completely upon Him.

As the exhausted traveler in the desert searches for the spring until he finds it to quench his burning thirst, so will the Christian who thirsts for the pure water of life obtain it of Christ—the fountain.

As we come to recognize the faultlessness of the character of the Savior we shall yearn to become totally changed and renewed in His image. As we learn more of God, our ideal of character becomes higher and our longing to reflect His likeness more earnest. When the soul gets in touch with God, a divine ingredient is merged with the human and we can say with David—

> My soul, wait only upon God and silently submit
> to Him; for my hope and expectation are from Him.
> Psalm 12:15

The hungering and thirsting after righteousness is an indication that Christ has performed a work upon the heart. The purpose of this work is to bring the Christian, to the point of seeking Christ, to do for him through the endowment of the Holy Spirit, the things which are impossible for him to do for himself. If we will rise higher in our faith we will be able to drink freely of the great fountain of life.

The wellsprings of life are the words of God. All who feast on these living springs will be brought into communion with Christ. Their minds will be open and familiar teams will be presented with improved understanding. Scriptural topics will impact the mind with new meaning as a flash of light. The relation of other truths will be made clear to the work of redemption. What rejoicing there will be in the soul to know that Christ is leading you. He is the divine Teacher who will remain at your side to teach you all things.

> But whoever takes a drink of water that I will give
> him shall never, no never be thirsty any more. But the
> water that I will give him shall become a spring of
> water welling (flowing, bubbling) [continually] within
> him unto (into, for) eternal life. John 4:14

"As the Holy Spirit opens to you the truth you will treasure up the most precious experiences and will long to speak to others of the comforting things that have been revealed to you. When brought into association with them you will communicate some fresh thought in regard to the character of the work of Christ. You will have some fresh revelation of His pitying love to impact to those who love Him and to those who love Him not." Thoughts From the Mount of Blessing p. 20

Jesus said, Give, and [gifts] will be given to you; good measure, pressed down, shaken together, and running over, . . . For with the measure you deal out [with the measure you use when you confer benefits on others], it will be measured back to you. Luke 6:38

The heart that has experience the love of Christ will continually cry out for deeper insights into the ways of God. As he imparts to others that which he has received, he will be given a richer and more abundant measure. Every disclosure of God to the soul will amplify the ability and capacity to know and to love. The heart will cry out "More of thee O God," and the Holy Spirit's response shall be "Much more."

Ephesians 3:20 states:

> Now to Him who, by (in consequence of) the [action of His] power that is at work within us, is able to [carry out His purpose and] do superabundantly, far over and above all that we [dare] ask or think [infinitely beyond our highest prayers, desires, thought hopes, or dreams].

The Holy Spirit will be given to every child of God when the whole heart is surrendered for Him to indwell. He commands his people—"Be filled and stimulated with the [Holy] Spirit." Eph. 5:18. Jesus Himself was filled with the Holy Spirit when He emptied Himself for the salvation of lost humanity.

Colossians 1:19 says:

> For it has pleased [the Father] that all the divine fullness (the Sum total of the divine perfection, powers, and attributes) should dwell in Him permanently.

Discover now your place through Christ:
Colossians 2:10 says of you,

> And you are in Him, made full and having come
> to fullness of life [in Christ you too are filled with the
> Godhead—Father, Son and Holy Spirit—and reach
> full spiritual stature]. And He is the Head of all rule
> and authority [of every angelic principality and power].

The perfection of Christ is our to achieve through His power. It is available to bring us into completeness in Him. As the wisdom of God is received we become wise. Through constant consistent communion with Him the Divine nature becomes imbedded in the soul. This spiritual union will produce everything that is need for this life and for eternity.

God has and will pour out His love permanently, as showers of rain that refresh the earth. He says:

> Let rain fall in showers, you heavens, from above,
> and let the skies rain down righteousness, [the pure,
> spiritual, heaven-born possibilities that have their
> foundation in the holy being of God]; let the earth
> open, and let them [skies and earth] sprout forth
> salvation, and let righteousness germinate and spring
> up [as plants do] together; I the Lord have created it.
> Isa. 45:8 Amp
>
> The poor and needy are seeking water when there
> is none; their tongues are parched with thirst. I the
> Lord will answer them; I, the God of Israel, will not
> forsake them. I will open rivers on the bare heights,
> and fountains in the midst of the valleys; I will make
> the wilderness a pool of water, and the dry land springs
> of water. Isa. 41:17-18

God is declaring His ability to provide for His people.

> For out of His fullness (abundance) we have all received [all had a share and we were all supplied with] one grace after another and spiritual blessing upon spiritual blessing and even favor upon favor and gift [heaped] upon gift. John 1:16 Amp

The Christian who hungers and thirst after righteousness will be filled with abundant life and eternal life. God says that he shall have:

Goodness and Knowledge

> Personally I am satisfied about you, my brethren, that you yourselves are rich in goodness, amply filled with all [spiritual] knowledge and competent to admonish and counsel and instruct one another also. Romans 15:14

The fullness of God

> [That you may really come] to know [practically, through experience for yourselves] the love of Christ, which far surpasses mere knowledge [without experience]; that you may be filled [through all your being] unto the fullness of God [may have the richest measure of the divine Presence, and become a body wholly filled and flooded with God himself]! Ephesians 3:19

The fruits of righteousness

> May you abound in and be filled with the fruits of righteousness (of right standing with God and

right doing) which comes through Jesus Christ (the Anointed One), to the honor and praise of God [that His glory may be both manifested and recognized]. Philippians 1:11

Knowledge and discernment of God's will

For this reason we also, from the day we heard of it, have not ceased to pray and make [special] request for you, [asking] that you may be filled with the full (deep and clear) knowledge of His will in all spiritual wisdom [in comprehensive insight into the ways and purposes of God] and in understanding and discernment of spiritual things—Colossians 1:9

Joy and the Holy Spirit

And the disciples were continually filled [throughout their souls] with joy and the Holy Spirit.

CHAPTER SIX

BE MERCIFUL

Key 5

Emulating the mercifulness of God.

Only the unselfish heart, the humble and trustful spirit, shall see God as "merciful and gracious, long-suffering, and abundant in goodness and truth." Exodus 34: 6

Merciful comes from the Greek word "eleemones" meaning to be pitiful, merciful, and compassionate, to have a forgiving spirit, empathy.

The Communicator's Commentary says:

The word carries the meaning of identification of suffering of others, of going through something with another, of entering into another's problem with understanding and acceptance. p. 64

Marvin R. Vincent says—

The word "Mercy" (eleos) emphasizes the misery with which grace deals, hence, the sense of human wretchedness coupled with the impules to relieve it, which issues in gracious ministry. Vincent's Word Studies In the New Testament. Vol. 1, p. 263

The Preacher's Outline and Sermon Bible defines Merciful (eleemones) as: to have a forgiving spirit and a compassionate heart. It is showing mercy and being benevolent. It is forgiving those who are wrong, yet it is much more. It is empathy; it is getting right inside the person and feeling right along with him. It is a deliberate effort, an act of the will to understand the person and to meet his need by forgiving and showing mercy. It is the opposite of being hard, unforgiving, and unfeeling.

The mercy of which Christ is speaking is an active outward virtue that is manifested in compassion on mans part toward man. It has no value until it is demonstrated in deeds of mercy. The greatest expression of mercy was given on behalf of man, and it took place on the cross of Calvary when God was in Christ reconciling the world unto Himself. Christ identified with humanity's suffering and paid the price for the sins of our race.

It is important to note that mercy is an essential quality of God. "Blessed be the God and Father of our Lord Jesus Christ, the Father of sympathy (pity and mercy) and the God [who is the source] of every comfort (consolation and encouragement)." 1 Cor. 1:3 But God—so rich is He in His mercy! Because of, and in order to, satisfy the great and wonderful and intense love with which He loved us. Ephesians 2: 4 Amp.

Mercy is an attribute of God that is communicated to men. Due to this fact Jesus commands: "so be merciful (sympathetic, tender, responsive, and compassionate) even as your Father is [all these]." Luke 6: 36 Amp.

By nature the heart of man is unloving, dark and cold. Whenever we manifest a spirit of forgiveness and mercy, we do it not of ourselves, but through the influence of the Holy Spirit working on our heart. I John 4:19 says, "We love, because He first loved us." R.V.

The source of all mercy is God. His name is "merciful and gracious" Exodus 34:6 says;

> "And the Lord passed by before him, and proclaimed, The Lord, The Lord God, merciful and gracious, slow to anger, and abundant in loving-kindness and truth."

God does not treat us according to our deadness. He does not ask if we are worthy of His love. Being Himself, the source of love He pours upon us the richness of His love, to make us worthy. He does not seek to get back at us or to punish us, but to redeem us. Christ seeks with intense desire to eradicate our woes and to apply His healing balms to our wounds.

The merciful are partaking of the divine nature, for in them the compassionate love of God is exhibited. When the heart is in sympathy with the heart of Infinite Love it will seek to reclaim ailing humanity to God. The soul becomes a spring of living water when Christ is dwelling there. Where He abides, there is no lack, there will always be an overflow of beneficence.

We come into contact daily with the erring, those who are tempted, those who fall victims to want and sin. They are all around and among us—in the work place, in our schools, on the streets, in the parks, in our neighborhoods, in our churches, and in our families and friends. To this group the Christian will ask, how can I benefit you? How can I be a blessing to you? These are those for whom Christ died to save. It was for these that God has given to us His children, the ministry of reconciliation.

The merciful manifest's compassion to the poor, the suffering and the oppressed. We discover a great example, in the testimony of Job:

> Because I delivered the poor that cried, and the fatherless, and him that had none to help him. The blessing of him that was ready to perish came upon me, and I caused the widow's heart to sing for joy. I put on righteousness, and it clothed me: my judgment was as a robe and a diadem. I was eyes to the blind, and feet was I to the lame. I was a father to the poor: and the cause which I knew not I searched out. Job 29:12-16
>
> "There are many to whom life is a painful struggle, they feel their deficiencies and are miserable and unbelieving, they think they have nothing for which to be grateful. Kind words, looks of sympathy, expressions of appreciation, would be to many a struggling and lonely one, as the cup of cold water to a thirsty soul. A word of sympathy, an act of kindness, would lift burdens that rest heavily upon weary shoulders. And every word or deed of unselfish kindness is an expression of the love of Christ for lost humanity." Thought From the Mount of Blessing p. 23

David said in Psalm 41:1-3

> Blessed (happy, fortunate, to be envied) is he who considers the weak and the poor; the Lord will deliver him in the time of evil and trouble. The Lord will protect him and keep him alive, he shall be called blessed in the land; and You will not deliver him to

the will of his enemies. The Lord will sustain, refresh, and strengthen him on his bed of languishing; all his bed You [O Lord] will turn, change, and transform in his illness.

The Christian who gives himself to God in ministry to his fellow men is joined with Him who has an unlimited supply of resources at his command. The Lord will never forsake or fail him in the hour of his suffering or need."

Philippians 4:19 states:

And my God will liberally supply (fill to the full) your every need according to His riches in glory in Christ Jesus.

The merciful live with the glorious promise that in the hour of his final need he shall find refuge and mercy in his compassionate Saviour who shall receive him into everlasting habitations.

God calls all believers to practice mercy:
They care for the poor.
Isaiah 58:6-7

[Rather] is not this the fast that I have chosen: to loose the bonds of wickedness, to undo the bonds of the yoke, to let oppressed go free, and that you break every [enslaving] yoke! Is it not to divide your bread with the hungry and bring the homeless poor into your house—when you see the naked, that you cover him, and that you hid not yourself from [the needs of] your own flesh and blood?

Compassionate to the afflicted
Job 16:14

> To him who is about to faint and despair, kindness
> is due from his friends, lest he forsake the fear of the
> Almighty.

Comfort with words
Job 16:5

> [But] I would strengthen and encourage with [the
> words of] my mouth and the consolation of my lips
> would soothe your suffering.

Bearing burdens of others
Galatians 6:2

> Bear (endure, carry) one another's burdens and
> troublesome moral faults, and in this way fulfill and
> observe perfectly the law of Christ (the Messiah) and
> complete what is lacking [in your obedience to it].

Through the demonstration of mercy, the children of God are called upon to bear the weight, the burden, the heaviness of their fellow man. The golden rule—"Whatever you would that men should do to you, do ye even so to them" (Matt. 7:12) commands every follower of Christ to reflect on another person problems as if there were his own. If this principle is strictly practice in personal relationships, in the home, in the community, in the school, in the church, in our nation and all nations around the world, we will solve the ills of the universe. It is only the grace of Christ that can enable us to apply this principle under every circumstance.

Christ's life was driven by the principle of bearing others burdens. He came to earth to be men's burden bearer. He commanded His disciples to love one another. In His teaching He declared that all the law and the prophets—all of the revealed will of God—are based on love. Love toward God and toward one's fellow men. Indeed love fulfills the law.

Restoring the falling
Galatians 6:1

> Brethren, if any person is overtaken in misconduct or sin of any sort, you who are spiritual [who are responsive to and controlled by the Spirit] should set him right and restore

Paul is here bringing out the practical reality of Christianity. It is possible that a Christian in a moment of weakness to be taken off guard, and become tripped up by temptation. The child of God does not practice or take pleasure in sin, however, to his dismay he may discover the weakness of the flesh. When a brother falls into sin, then who are spiritual are commissioned to reach out in mercy to restore the fallen.

The function of those who are spiritual is to mend, to restore and to put back in shape the one that has sinned. The spiritual one is not to take an attitude of self-importance toward his brother who has fallen to temptation. He must not be discouraged, criticized, or censure to aggravate him to indulge further in the works of the flesh. He stands in need of a sympathetic hand to help him out of the pit of sin into which he had fallen. In this state he needs a brother to minister to him with patience, kindness and greatness. Someone with a humble attitude who realizes that he might himself someday be taken down by temptation and will stand in need of help.

Jesus is our example of meekness. Those who follow this example will be kind and long-suffering in dealing with their brethren. "They will not be critical and faultfinding, nor will they make haste to bring down upon one who errs the discipline of the church. Their zeal for justice will be seasoned with mercy. Their primary objective will be the restoration of the offender. Their proposals and decisions will be remedial, not punitive. The maintenance of church authority will be a secondary consideration." SDA Bible Commentary vol. 6 p. 984-985

Caring for physical needs
James 2:15-16

> If a brother or sister is poorly clad and lacks food for each day; and one of you says to him, Goodbye! Keep [yourself] warm and well fed, without giving him the necessities for the body what good does that do?

Supporting the weak
Acts 20:35

> In everything I have pointed out to you [by example] that, by working diligently in this manner, we ought to assist the weak, being mindful of the words of the Lord Jesus, how He Himself, said, "It is more blessed (makes one happier and more to be envied) to give than to receive."

God takes great delight in those who show mercy. When we exercise showing mercy we imitate God in the strongest way we possibly can. The Bible is filled with countless proofs of God's mercy to us. Every day of our lives we become the recipient of this undeserved mercy. In gratitude for his mercy we need to be merciful. "Our world is full of guilt and woe, which we may help to relieve, and every day of our lives we have opportunity by helping the poor and wretched, and by forgiving those who injure us, to show that we are like God." Albert Barnes Notes, p. 43

God will bestow abundant rewards to those who are merciful.

2 Samuel 22:26

> Toward the loving and loyal You will show Yourself loving and loyal, and with the upright and blameless You will show Yourself upright and blameless.

Psalms 18:25

> With the kind and merciful You will show Yourself kind and merciful, with an upright man You will show Yourself upright.

Receiving what has been given
Proverbs 19:17

> He who has pity on the poor lends to the Lord, and that which he has given He will repay to him.

Psalms 51:1

> Have mercy upon me O God, according to Your steadfast love; according to the multitude of Your tender mercy and loving-kindness blot out my transgression.

Have mercy in the end
2 Timothy 1:18

> May the Lord grant to him that he may find mercy from the Lord on that [great] day! And you know how many things he did for me and what a help he was at Ephesus [you know better that I can tell you].

Matthew 25:31-40—makes the point that the test of admission in the kingdom of God is deeds of mercy.

> When the Son of man comes in His glory (His majesty and splendor), and the Holy angels with Him, then He will sit on the throne of His glory. All nations will be gathered before Him, and he will separate them [the people] from one another as a shepherd separates his sheep from the goats; and He will cause the sheep to stand at His right hand, but the goats at His left. Then the King will say to those at His right hand, come, you blessed of My Father [you favored of God and appointed to eternal salvation], inherit (receive as your own) the Kingdom prepared for you from the foundation of the world. For I was hungry and you gave Me food, I was thirsty and you gave Me something to drink, I was a stranger and you brought me together with yourselves and welcomed and entertained and lodged Me, I was naked and you clothed Me, I was sick and you visited Me with help and ministering care, I was in prison and you came to see Me. Then the just and upright will answer Him, Lord, when did we see You hungry and gave You food, or thirsty and gave Your something to drink? And when did we see You a stranger and welcomed and entertained You, or naked and clothed You? And when did we see

You sick or in prison and came to visit You? And the King will reply to them, "Truly I tell you, in so far as you did it for one of the least [in the estimation of me] of these My brethren, you did it for Me." Matt. 25:31-40

Jesus gives a strong warning to those who are unmerciful.
Matthew 6:12, 14-15

And forgive us our debts, as we also have forgiven (left, remitted, and let go of the debts, and have given up resentment against) our debtors.

For if you forgive people their trespasses [their reckless and willful sins, leaving them, letting them go, and giving up resentment], your heavenly Father will also forgive you. But if you do not forgive others their trespasses [their reckless and willful sins, leaving them, letting them go, and giving up resentment], neither will your Father forgive you your trespasses.

"He who is unwilling to forgive others does not deserve to be forgiven. Furthermore, to extend forgiveness to him would be to condone his own unforgiving spirit. To expect of others what one is unwilling to do himself is the very essence of selfishness and sin. God's unwillingness to forgive one who harbors an unforgiving spirit is based on the need of the unforgiving person to overcome a basic character defect. God could not forgive such a person and at the same time be true to His own righteous character. Only when we are right with our fellow men can we be right with God." SDA Bible Commentary vol. 5 p. 348

Matthew 18:34-35

And in wrath his master turned him over to the torturers (the jailers), till he should pay all that he owed. So also My heavenly Father will deal with every one of you if you do not freely forgive your brother from your heart his offenses.

Taking into account God's infinite mercy to us, it behooves us to show mercy to others. When we refuse to extend forgiveness to others we block the channel whereby to receive our own forgiveness. In light of this, we need to think and consider how God has treated us in our circumstances before we seek to accuse others and demand justice. The Christian, therefore, will reflect on the mercy of God toward him and do likewise toward his fellow men. This is our ideal standard in dealing with our fellow men.

Repeating the words I forgive you, essential they may be, are not of most importance before God. It is the attitude of the heart from where the words came. A pretense forgiveness prompted by circumstance or for ulterior reasons may deceive the hearer, but it cannot fool Him who is able to read the heart. Forgiveness is a central aspect of Christian perfection.

James 2:13

> For to him who has shown no mercy the judgment [will be] merciless, but mercy [full of glad confidence] exalts victoriously our judgment.

Un-forgiveness darkens the soul, stains the life, negatively influence the action and leads to self destruction and death. Forgiveness on the other hand lifts the spirit, brightens the disposition and brings the life into harmony with the will of God. The heart practices unconditional forgiveness thus becoming pure as He is pure. The pure in heart are blessed and have the glorious assurance of seeing God.

CHAPTER SEVEN

BE PURE IN HEART

Key 6

Pure in heart

Every impure thought defiles the soul, impairs the moral sense, and wipes out the impressions of the Holy Spirit. The spiritual vision becomes dim, till man cannot look upon God. All impurity of speech or thought must be forsaken by those who are seeking to have clear discernment of spiritual truth.

To be pure (katharoi) refers to one who is honest, unmixed, unpolluted, sincere, unsoiled, being holy, and having single purpose, without hypocrisy.

The word translated heart designates—
1. The intellect—Matthew 13:15

> For this nation's heart has grown gross (fat and dull), and their ears heavy and difficult of hearing. And their eyes they have lightly closed, lest they see and perceive with their eyes, and hear and comprehend the sense with their ears, and grasp and understand with their heart, and turn and I should heal them.

2. The conscience—I John 3:20, 21

> Whenever our hearts in [tormenting] self accusation make us feel guilty and condemn us. [For we are God's hands.] For He is above and greater than our consciences (our hearts), and He knows (perceives and understands) everything [nothing is hidden from Him]. Amp.
>
> And, beloved, if our conscience (our hearts) do not accuse us [if they do not make us feel guilty and condemn us], we have confidence (complete assurance and boldness) before God.

3. The inner man—1 Peter 3:4

> But let it be the inward adorning and beauty of the hidden person of the heart, with the incorruptible and unfading charm of a gentle and peaceful spirit, which [it is not anxious or wrought up, but] is very precious in the sight of God.

    a. Feelings
    b. Emotions

c. Purposes

d. Motives

e. Intentions

In the time of Jesus the Jews were so precise in regard to ceremonial purity that their instructions were tremendously oppressive. They were possessed with rules and regulations and the fear of outward adulterations that they did not recognize the blemish that self-centeredness left on their souls.

Nowhere does Jesus mention ceremonial purity as one of the conditions of entering into the Kingdom. He did, however, pointed to the need of being pure in heart.

James 3:17 says:

> But the wisdom from above is first of all pure (undefiled); then it is peace-loving, courteous (considerate, gentle). [It is willing to] yield to reason, full of compassion and good fruits; it is wholehearted and straight forward, impartial and unfeigned (free from doubts, wavering, and insincerity).

It seems here that James had come to the realization that the believers had not yet attained the desired goal of Christian maturity. He takes time to explain how they may find the power and understanding that will make them victorious Christians amid the problems of life. In Ch, 1:5 he points out that wisdom "Sophia" means "broad and full intelligence. This takes into account more than true knowledge alone does not give assurance of right action or even right conclusions. Wisdom prompts us to put proper value on the many things that competes for our attention. It ensures the accurate use of knowledge as right actions are sought for.

Wisdom is to be continuously sought in order to meet each new test of faith and endurance successfully. Problems of life, though common to all men, are baffling to those who cannot face them from the Christian viewpoint. To live life as God designed, we need to receive a daily supply of heavenly wisdom. For all who ask in sincerity is first pure—"free from defilement." This quality is first in the order given here by James because the qualities that follow it grow out of an undefiled, "God given philosophy of life." The wisdom is free the principles, pursuits and goals of everything earthly. It comes from God, it is pure and is available to those who ask for it.

The true wisdom which God guarantees for all who ask in sincerity is first pure—"free from defilement." This quality is first in the order given here by James because the qualities the follow it grow out of an undefiled, "God given philosophy of life."

God will allow nothing that is defiled to enter into His Kingdom. All who shall inherit the city of God will have on this earth become pure in heart. They will have and now be growing into the image of Jesus. There will be developed in them a progressive dislike for carelessness, unacceptable language and degrading thoughts. Christ will be abiding in the heart, and where He abides there will be purity of thought and manner.

Jesus says in Matthew 15:11, 18-20

It is not what goes into the mouth of a man that makes him unclean and defiled, but what comes out of the mouth; that makes a man unclean and defiles [him]. But whatever comes out of the mouth comes from the heart, and this is what makes a man unclean and defiles [him]. For out of the heart comes evil thoughts (reasoning and disputing and designs) such as murder, adultery, sexual vice, theft, false witnessing, slander, and irreverent speech. These are what make a man unclean and defile [him], but eating with unwashed hands does not make him unclean or defile [him]. Amp.

One of the functions of the mouth is eating. Through eating man takes in that which is needed to give sustenance to the body. What goes into the mouth, Jesus says, does not make me unclean, defiled or impure. It is what comes out of the mouth that attention must be placed on, for it is what comes out of the mouth, makes a man unclean, defiled or impure. Why is this a fact? Because "out of the abundance (overflow) of the heart his mouth speaks" (Luke 6:45).

The heart that is pure will reflect to the world in the quality of his character what God is like. Jesus points out a pattern of perfection that the pure in heart will adopt and cultivate as a way of life. He says thus:

> Ye have heard that it hath been said, Thou shalt love thy neighbor, and hate thine enemy. But I say unto you, love your enemies, bless them that curse you, do good to them that hate you, and pray for them which despitefully use you, and persecute you; That ye may be the children of your Father which is in heaven; for he maketh his sun to rise on the evil and on the good, and sendeth rain on the just and on the unjust. For it ye love them which love you, what reward have ye? Do even the publicans the same? And if ye salute your brethren only, what do ye more than others? Do not even the publicans so? Be ye therefore perfect, even as your Father which is in heaven is perfect. Matthew 5: 43-48 KJV

Jesus is here calling His followers to the highest and truest form of love. This type of love drives men to sacrifice themselves for others. It entails reverence for God and respect for our fellow men. "It is a divine principle of thought and action that modifies the character, governs the impulse, controls the passions and enables the affections." (SDA Bible Commentary vol. 5 p. 340) This standard of love can only be experienced by those who are pure in heart.

In the time of Jesus, the Jews accepted only fellow Israelite as neighbors. Even their half-breed relatives—the Samaritans were considered strangers. This narrow concept was brushed away by Jesus who proclaimed the "brotherhood, or neighborhood, of all men." Pure love seeks the good of all men without consideration for race or creed. Harboring hatred or contempt for others is natural of self and pride, and evident that he heart is impure. To love our enemies is to treat them with respect and courtesy—the same way we want to be treated—and to look upon them as God looks at them.

The pure in heart are the "sons of their Heavenly Father." They resemble Him in character. Their test of love is love for their fellow men.—If anyone says, I love God, and hates (detests, abominates) his brother [in Christ], he is a liar; for he who does not love his brother, whom he has seen, cannot love God, whom he has not seen. (I John 4:20) It is valuable to understand that the inner attitudes and motives determine perfection of character—the pureness of the heart—and not the outward acts only. Man looks on the outward appearance, but God looks on the heart (I Sam. 16:7). To be children of our Father in heave, we must be perfect and pure in heart even as our Father is heaven is perfect and pure.

Jesus is he speaking of purity that goes far beyond sexual purity. He is speaking about heart purity, the inward cleanness of the heart. This includes:

(1) Ridding oneself of all traits of character that are undesirable.

Galatians 5:19-21 says:

> Now the doings (practices) of the flesh are clear (obvious); they are immorality, impurity, indecency,

idolatry, sorcery, enmity, strife, jealousy, anger (ill temper), selfishness, divisions (dissensions), party spirit (factions, sects with peculiar opinions heresies), envy, drunkenness, carousing, and the like. I warn you beforehand, just as I did previously, that those who do such things shall not inherit the Kingdom of God. Amp.

(2) The development of all the desirable character traits of the Lord. Galatians 5:22-23 shows:

But the fruit of the (Holy) Spirit [the work which his presence within accomplishes] is love, joy (gladness), peace, patience, (an even temper, forbearing), kindness, goodness (benevolence), faithfulness, gentleness, (meekness, humility), self-control (self-restraint, continence). Against such things is no law [that can bring a change].

Certainly the pure in heart are children of God who have made a conscious decision to have their lives governed by the Holy Spirit of God.

Galatians 5:24-25

And those who belong to Christ Jesus (the Messiah) have crucified the flesh (the godless human nature) with its passions and appetites and desires. If we live by the (Holy) Spirit, let us also walk by the Spirit. [If by the Holy Spirit we have our life in God, let us go forward walking in line, our conduct controlled by the Spirit].

The pure in heart has forsaken sin as a governing principle of the life. The life is lived totally consecrated to God.

Romans 6:14-16 says:

> For sin shall not [any longer] exert dominion over you, since now you are not under law [as slaves], but under grace [as subjects of God's favor and mercy]. What then [are we to conclude]? Shall we sin because we live not under the law but under God's favor and mercy? Certainly not! Do you not know that if you continually surrender yourselves to anyone to do his will, you are the slaves of him whom you obey, whether that be to sin, which leads to death, or to obedience which leads to righteousness (right doing and right standing with God)?

To be pure in the heart does not mean that the child of God is absolutely sinless. It means, however, that the motives are right, and by the grace of God abiding in him, he turns his back on past mistakes. He is now pressing forward toward perfection in Christ Jesus.

Philippians 3:13-15

> Brethren, I count not myself to have apprehended; but this one thing I do forgetting those things which are behind, and reaching forth unto those things which are before, I press toward the mark for the prize of the high calling of God in Christ Jesus. Let us therefore, as many as be perfect, be thus minded; and if in anything ye be otherwise minded, God shall reveal even this unto you. (KJV)

The pure in heart will live a clean life, "keeping himself unspotted from the world." (James 1:27).

Bring into play all the powers of the will he ventures to serve his master depending totally on Him for his very life." I do not ask that You take them out of the world, but that You will keep and protect them from the evil one." (Jn. 17:15) "Now unto Him that is able to keep you from falling and to present you faultless before the presence of his glory." (Jude 24) Only he who unites his human effort with the power of the omnipotent God will have success in the Christian life.

Jesus teaches that the pure in heart will see God. In this He places emphasis on the kingdom of divine grace in the hearts of men in this present age, but not to the exclusion of the kingdom of eternal glory that is to come. The phase "see God" is used with a two-fold meaning. It refers to spiritual sight as well as, physical sight.

"Those who feel their spiritual need enter the "kingdom of heaven" (v3) now; those who mourn for sin (v4) are comforted now; those who are humble hearted (v5) receive their title to the new earth now; those who hunger and thirst after the righteousness of Jesus Christ (v6) are filled now; the merciful (v7) obtain mercy now. In like manner, the pure in heart have the privilege of seeing God now, through eyes of faith; and eventually, in the glorious Kingdom, it will be their privilege to see Him face to face." SDA Bible Commentary vol. 5 p. 327

1 John 3:2 states:

> Beloved, we are [even here and] now God's children; it is not yet disclosed (made clear) what we shall be [hereafter], but we know that when he comes and is manifested, we shall [as God's children] resemble and be like Him, for we shall see Him just as He [really] is. Amp.

Sinners cannot and will not see God. The devil blinds and persuades them into believing that by experimenting with sin they will have clearer vision. Sin, however, leads them further into blindness. Sinners have eyes but they cannot see.

Jeremiah 5:21 states:

> Hear now this, O foolish people without understanding or heart, who have eyes and see not, who have ears and hear not!

Those who will see God are those with singleness of heart. When the eye of the soul is single the life will be full of light.

> The eye is the lamp of the body. So if our eye is sound, your entire body will be full of light. But if your eye is unsound, your whole body will be full of darkness. If then the very light in you [your conscience] is darkened, how dense is that darkness? Matthew 6:22-23 Amp.

The only safety we have is to live by the principle of making God first in our life. The eyes of our soul must be kept clean if we desire to see God. When through the eyes of faith the beauty and glory of God are seen the heart will yearn to be at peace with Him and to be a channel of this peace to the world.

———— •———

CHAPTER EIGHT

CULTIVATE TRUE PEACE

Key 7

Peace-making

The one power that can establish perpetuate true peace is the grace of Christ. When this peace in imbedded in the heart, it will extinguish the evil passion that create strife and dissension.

The Greek word "eirenopoioi" from which we get "peacemaker" is composed of two words "eirene"—peace and "poieo",— to make. The word literally means peace-maker, "It implies" not merely making peace between those who are at variance, but working peace as that which is the will of the God of peace for men." W.L. Walker

In this teaching Christ is referring particularly to bringing men into harmony with God. This peace that comes from Christ is born in truth and is harmony with God. The world, however, is at enmity with the law of God. Romans 8:7 say:

[That is] because the mind of the flesh [with its carnal thoughts and purposes] is hostile to God, for it does not submit itself to God's Law; indeed it cannot.

Sinners are at enmity with their Maker, and because of this they are at enmity with each other. Peace cannot be manufactured by men. Human plans for the purification and uplifting of individuals or of society will fail of producing peace because they do not reach the heart. The only power that can create or perpetuate true peace is the grace of Christ. When this is implanted in the heart, it will cast out the evil passions that cause strife and dissension." Desire of Ages. 303

For you shall go out [from the spiritual exile caused by sin and evil into the homeland] with joy and be led forth [by your Leader, the Lord Himself, and His word] with peace; the mountain and the hills shall break forth before you into singing, and all the trees of the field shall clap their hands. Instead of the thorn shall come up the cypress tree, and instead of the brier shall come up the myrtle tree . . . . The wilderness and the dry land shall be glad; the desert shall rejoice and blossom like the rose and the autumn crocus. Isa. 55:12-13; 35:1

The psalmist declares in Psalm 119:165

> Great peace have they who love Your law; nothing
> shall offend them or make them stumble. Amp.

Jesus Christ is The Prince of Peace

> For to us a child is born, to us a Son is given;
> and the government shall be upon his shoulder; and
> his name shall be called Wonderful, Counselor, The
> mighty God, The everlasting Father, The Prince of
> Peace. Of the increase of his government and peace

there shall be no end, upon the throne of David, and upon his Kingdom, to order it, and to stablish it with judgment and with justice from henceforth even forever. The zeal of the Lord of hosts will perform this. Isa. 9:6-7 KJV

Being the Prince of Peace, Christ came to earth on a mission to restore the peace that sin has broken. Romans 5:1 says:

Therefore, since we are justified (acquitted, declared righteous, and given a right standing with God) through faith, let us [grasp the fact that we] have [the peace of reconciliation to hold and to enjoy] peace with God through our Lord Jesus Christ (the Messiah, the Anointed One). Amp.

The only way to experience this peace is to make a conscience decision to renounce sin in all its forms. Next the heart must be open to receive and experience the love of Christ. With Christ's love ruling the life from the heart, one becomes a partaker of the heavenly peace.

"There is no other ground of peace than this. The grace of Christ received into the heart, subdues enmity; it allays strife and fills the soul with love. He who is at peace with God and his fellow men cannot be made miserable. Envy will not be in his heart; evil surmising will find no room there; hatred cannot exist. The heart that is in harmony with God is a partaker of the peace of heaven and will diffuse its blessed influence on all around. The spirit of peace will rest like dew upon hearts weary and troubled with worldly strife." Thought From the Mount of Blessing, p. 29

"In order to appreciate what Christ meant when He spoke of "peacemakers" it is helpful to take note of the meaning of peace in Semitic thinking and speech. The Hebrew equivalent of the Greek eirene is shalom, meaning "completeness," "soundness," "prosperity," "condition of well-being," "peace." In view of the fact that Christ and the common people used Aramaic; a language closely akin to the Hebrew, Jesus doubtless used the word with its Semitic connotations. Christians are to be at peace among themselves (I Thess. 5:13) and to follow peace with all men (Heb. 12:14). They are to pray for peace, to work or peace, and to take a constructive interest in activities that contribute to a peaceful state of society." SDA Bible Commentary vol. 5 p. 328

When the Prince of Peace came to the end of His mission on earth, and was about to return to His Father, He left something of Himself with His followers. "My peace," He said, "I now give to you." This is one of the greatest gifts that has ever been given to men. Everyone who has been called to be an ambassador of peace, to go into the world taking peace, must have peace. "With it the World can be won, without it nothing can be done."

John 14:27 states:

> Peace I leave with you; My [own] peace I now give and bequeath to you. Not as the world gives do I give to you. Do not let your hearts be troubled, neither let them be afraid. [Stop allowing yourselves to be agitated and disturbed; and do not permit yourselves to be fearful and intimidated and cowardly and unsettled.] Amp.

As Christ's followers, Christians are sent into the world with the message of peace. "Whoever, by the quiet, unconscious influence of a holy life, shall reveal the love of Christ; whoever, by word or deed, shall lead another to renounce sin and yields his heart to God, is a peacemaker." Thought From the Mount of Blessing, p. 29

The first course of peace-makers is to have peace. Jesus says, "Peace I leave with you; My [own] peace I now give and bequeath to you."

(John 14:27) This peace must be accepted into the life, influence the mannerism and touch all with the warmth of God's love.

"But if you seek to live a pure and holy life, to learn daily in the school of Christ the lessons that He has invited you to learn, to be meek and lowly in heart, then you have a peace which no worldly circumstance can change. A life in Christ is a life of restfulness. Uneasiness, dissatisfaction, and restlessness reveal the absence of the Savior. If Jesus is brought into the life, that life will be filled with good and noble works for the Master. You will forget to be self-serving, and will live closer and still closer to the dear Savior; your character will become Christ-like, and all around you will take knowledge that you have been with Jesus and learned of Him. Testimonies vol. 5 p. 487

There are four areas of peace making.

1. Peace-makers make peace with God.

> For He is [Himself] our peace (our bond of unity and harmony), He has made us both [Jew and Gentile] one body, and has broken down (destroyed, abolished) the hostile dividing wall between us. By abolishing in His [own crucified] flesh the enmity [caused by] the Law with its decrees and ordinances [which He annulled], that He from the two might create in Himself one new man [one new quality of humanity out of the two], so making peace. And [He designed] to reconciled to God both [Jews and Gentile, united] in a single body by means of His cross, thereby killing the mutual enmity and bringing the feud to an end. And He came and preached the glad tidings of peace to you who were afar and [peace] to those who were near. (Eph. 2:14-17) Amp.

How can fallen men who have no peace make peace with God? It is not left to men to be the peacemaker, for he cannot give that which he does possess. Christ is not only the peacemaker; He is Himself peace, "the connection of union and peace. In Him all of the separations of humanity are done away with. The idea of peace in the Old Testament was linked with that of the Messiah. So by being their peace before God, Christ achieved peace between Jew and Gentile.

Paul says there is [now no distinction] neither Jew nor Greek, there is neither slave nor free, there is not male and female; for you are all one in Christ Jesus. (Gal. 3:28) By giving Himself a sacrifice on the cross, Christ broke down the partition wall that sustained the enmity between the nations, by abolishing the "law of commandments contained in ordinances."

"It is time that the ceremonial law came to an end at the cross, but it should be remembered that the ceremonial system as God gave it did not create the enmity Paul here describes. It was the interpretation the Jews placed upon it, the additions they made to it, and the exclusive and hostile attitudes they adapted as a result, that were the basis of the hostility. The added regulations, together with the involved interpretations, served either to modify the force and function of the original commands or else greatly to nullify them. Any Gentile who wished to join the "commonwealth of Israel" was confronted with an involved system of legal requirement. It is easy the Jewish system thus stood as an insurmountable barrier, a partition wall, preventing the Gentiles from accepting the worship of the true God. The Jews loathed and detested their Gentile neighbors, and the Gentiles, in turn, hated and despised their Jewish neighbors. God had entrusted the Jews with the divine "oracles" (Rom. 3:2). They stood in the world as the official representatives of the true religion. Until the founding of the Christian church there was no other people to whom God could direct the seekers for salvation." SDA Bible Commentary vol. 6 p. 1009)

In bringing peace, Christ has made of the two one new man. This goes beyond the harmony that He established between them. The

Greek word used here for new means new in quality rather than in time. He is now a new man, of different quality from either of the two elements composing him. The putting on of the new man or of the new nature is not an accomplishment we can attain of ourselves. This is by no means a refurbished man. God is active in the recreation of man, but the change is not effected apart from man's consent and cooperation. The new man is patterned according to God—after God—so since the new man is a return to man's original state, it is equivalent to the restoration of the image of God in the soul.

2. Peace-makers make peace with others.

> So let us definitely aim for an eagerly pursue what makes for harmony and for mutual up building (edification and development) for one another. (Roman 14:19) Amp.

True to his profession the peacemaker will do all he can do to build up the lives of those around him. He works to offer encouragement and comfort to the downhearted. Every opportunity given him is used to build up the spiritual lives of his brothers and sisters.

> Strive to live in peace with everybody and pursue that consecration and holiness without which no one will [ever] see the Lord. (Heb. 12:14)
> If possible, as far as it depends on you, live at peace with everyone. (Roman 12:18)

As far as the Christian is concerned, he is to do everything as though it depends on him to maintain peace. It must be noted, however, that at times circumstances will arise in which the Christian will have no control over what is taking place. In such cases he is to do all that he can do understanding that it is not always possible to make peace. He must, nevertheless make sure that wherever the peace is broken; it is not because of him.

One of the major instruments of destroying peace is the wrong use of the tongue. The tongue is responsible for destroying more lives them any other part of the body. It has destroyed friendships, marriages, families, churches, businesses, societies, nations and is wounding the world. The scripture has quite a bit to say about the tongue that will do us well to pay attention too.

Keep your tongue from evil and your lips from speaking deceit. Depart from evil and do good; seek, inquire for, and crave peace and pursue (go after) it! (Ps. 34:13)

The wise man Solomon said: Death and life are in the power of the tongue: and they that love it shall eat the fruit thereof. (Proverbs 18: 21 KJV) It is a fact that the tongue has discolored the reputation of many. It has even driven some to poverty even death. On the other hand, the tongue can be used for greatness. It can bring honor to God and blessing to men. It can encourage cheer up, build up, give hope, and proclaim the gospel of the soon coming Savor. Those who give the tongue free reign doing harm in destroying others will have all that evil return to them some day. But I [Jesus] say unto you, that every idle word that men shall speak, they shall give account thereof in the Day of Judgment. (Matthew 12: 36) KJV

For in many things we offend all. If any man offend not in word, the same is a perfect man, and able also to bridle the whole body. Behold, we put bits in the horses mounts, that they obey us; and we turn about their whole body. Behold also the ships, which though they be so great are driven of fierce winds, yet are they turned about with a very small helm, whithersoever the governor listeth. Even so the tongue is a little member, and boasteth great things. Behold, how great a matter a little fire kindleth. And the tongue is a fire, a world of iniquity: so is the tongue amongst our members, that it defileth the whole body, and setteth on fire the course of nature; and it is set on fire of hell. For every kind of beasts, and of birds, and of serpent, and of things in the sea, is tamed, and hath been tamed of mankind: But the tongue can no man tame; it is an unruly evil, full of deadly poison. Therewith bless we God, even the Father; and therewith curse we men, which are made after the similitude of God. Out of the same mouth proceedeth blessing and cursing. My brethren, these things ought not so to be. James 3: 2-10 KJV

The apostle gave counsel to all who love life and desire to have good days. He says:

> For let him who wants to enjoy life and see good days [good—whether apparent or not] keep his tongue free from evil and his lips from guile (treachery, deceit). Let him turn away from wickedness and shun it, and let him do right. Let him search for peace (harmony; undisturbedness from fears, agitating passions, and moral conflicts) and seek it eagerly. [Do not merely desire peaceful relations with God, with your fellowmen, and with yourself, but pursue, go after them!] For the eyes of the Lord are upon the righteous (those who are upright and in right standing with God), and His ears are attentive to their prayer. But the face of the Lord is against those who practice evil [to oppose them, to frustrate, and defeat them]. 1 Peter 3: 10-12 Amp.

3. Peace-makers make peace between others.

If your brother says Jesus wrongs you, go and show him his fault, between you and him privately. If he listens to you, you have won back your brother. But if he does not listen, take along with you one or two others, so that every word may be confirmed and upheld by the testimony of two or three witnesses. (Matthew 18: 15-16 Amp.) Jesus is here teaching His followers how to preserve relationships. It is Christ-like that a brother should go privately to the one who wrong him and reestablish the peace that was lost. It was said by someone "the best way to dispose of our enemies is to make friends of them." To put into circulation the wrongs the brother may have done will make it difficult sometimes impossible to reach him. The chances of gaining the brother and regaining peace are always possible.

It must be kept in mind that the brother may or may not listen. In the event he does not listen Jesus teaches that one or two other persons should be taken on a second attempt of establishing peace. The "one or two" are not personal involved in the matter and are in a good position to give an unbiased opinion and counsel to the fallen brother. What a privilege it is to be called to make peace between those who have been split apart by some form of offence. The peace-maker must bear in mind that "the talent of influence is a sacred trust, one for which we will inevitable be called upon to give account in the day of judgment." SDA Bible Commentary vol. 5 p. 447

In the event the offending brother neglect to take the given admonition, witness can be given to the facts involve in the case and of the effort put forth to seek reestablishment of the relationship. It has been said that there are two sides to every story, and the truth is never known until there are reliable witnesses. As a witness the peace-maker must be mindful that he stands before God in service and must do all that he does as unto the Lord.

Do nothing from factional motives [through contentiousness, strife, selfishness, or for unworthy ends] or prompted by conceited and empty arrogance. Instead, in the true spirit of humility (lowliness and mind) let each regard the other as better than and superior to himself [thinking more highly of one another than you do yourselves]. Philippians 2: 3 Amp.

In the life of the Christian nothing should be from selfishness, selfish ambition, partisanship, empty pride, conceit and the like. Works done in such a spirit will have no lasting benefit. There will be no setting of goals or formulating of plans that is prompted by selfish ambition or a longing to outdo others. God is displeased if the motive is inspired by such evils.

When one takes it upon himself to judge another, he does it from his own point of view based on his experiences, way of life, likes and dislikes and so on. The humble peacemaker will be aware of his own defects realizing that he does not have the same comprehensive view of the defects of others.

"It is natural for those who have any just sense of the defects of their own souls to hope that it is not so with others and to believe that they have purer hearts. This leads them to feel that others are deserving of greater respect than themselves. A truly pious man will always be a humble man and will wish that others be preferred in office and honor. This will not make him blind to other's defects when they are manifested, but he will personally be modest and unobtrusive. This Christian standard rebukes inordinate love of office and helps to produce contentment wherever the providence of God may have cast our lot." SDA Bible Commentary vol. 7 p. 153

Behold, how good and how pleasant it is for brethren to dwell together in unity! It is like the precious ointment poured on the head, that ran down on the beard, even the beard of Aaron [the first high priest], that came down upon the collar and skirts of his garments [consecrating the whole body]. It is like the dew of [lofty] Mount Hermon and the dew that comes on the hills of Zion; for there the Lord has commanded the blessing, even life forever more [upon the high and the lowly]. Ps. 133 Amp.

4. Peace-makers make peace between man and God.

But all things are from God, who through Jesus Christ reconciled us to Himself [received us into favor, brought us into harmony with Himself] and give to us the ministry of reconciliation [that by word and deed we might aim to bring others into harmony with Him]. 2 Corinthians 5:18 Amp.

Our world was plunge into sin, sin brought alienation, alienation created a separation between God and man, and this gulf was bridged by Jesus Christ who introduces reconciliation. Reconciliation is to exchange or restore to favor. Through Christ man can now enjoy fellowship with God. Christ going to the cross was the greatest demonstration of the love of God toward mankind. God has always hated sin. He does not treat good and evil as equals. The atonement does not amend the law, it, however, changes the enmity that existed because of sin. Reconciliation removed the hostility by means of a substitutionary fulfillment of the law's requirements.

Now, Christians who were once separated from God are enjoying fellowship. Thanks be to Christ our Savior for reconciling us to the Father. In return every believer is called to reconcile others to God through Christ. It is the Christian purpose in taking up this ministry to lead lost humanity into fellowship with God.

Christ gave to the Christian church a command that we call today the Great Commission. Therein lies the command to reconcile men to God their Father. Jesus said: All authority (all power of rule) in heaven and on earth has been given to Me. Go then and make disciples of all nations, baptizing them into the name of the Father and of the Son and of the Holy Spirit, teaching them to observe everything that I have commanded you, and behold, I am with you all the days (perpetually, uniformly, and on every occasion), to the [very] close and consummation of the age. Amen (so let it be). Matthew 28:18-20 Amp.

Mark records:

> And He said to them, Go into all the world and preach and publish openly the good news (the Gospel) to every creature [of the whole human race]. He who believes [who adheres to and trusts in and relies on the Gospel and Him whom it sets forth] and is baptized will be saved [from the penalty of eternal death]; but he who does not believe [who does not adhere to and trust in and rely on the Gospel and Him whom it sets forth] will be condemned. And these attesting signs will accompany those who believe; in My name they will drive out demons; they will speak in new languages; they will pick up serpents; and [even] if they drink anything deadly, it will not hurt them; they will lay their hands on the sick, and they will get well. Mark 16:15-18 Amp.

All those who accept the proclamation of the gospel are presented with two requirements. The first—faith is Jesus Christ. This is the inward acceptance of the salvation that is provided by His atoning death on the cross. The second is baptism—which is an outward sign of that inward change of the life. A choice is here given to the world to accept Jesus and be saved or to disbelieve and walk in condemnation. The heart of the peace-maker is joined with the heart of God in desiring all men to be saved by coming to repentance. That decision, however, can only be made by man himself. With much prayer tears and effort man is encouraged to accept life and live.

It is the promise of Jesus that the work of the ones making peace shall be followed with supernatural and miraculous demonstrations of divine power. The word "miracle" is define by Webster as "an event or effect in the physical world deviating from the known laws of nature, or transcending our knowledge of these laws; an extraordinary, anomalous, or abnormal event brought about by superhuman agency." The same word is define by The Oxford English Dictionary as "a marvelous event occurring within human experience, which cannot have been brought about by human power or by the operation of any natural agency, and must therefore be ascribed to the special intervention of the Deity or of some supernatural being; chiefly, an act (e.g. of healing) exhibiting control over the laws of nature, and serving as evidence that the agent is either divine or is specially favoured by God."

The signs—miracles that Christ will perform through peace-makers will be done to supply genuine needs. Every one will be of a character as to lead sinful man unto Him who is the tree of life. "God is not honored in being called upon to do that which men are able to do for themselves. Only when men recognize that their needs are beyond human wisdom and skill to supply, can the ultimate purpose of a miracle be realized. Indeed, there must first be a profound sense of need. Next, there must be faith that God can and will supply the help so desperately needed. There must also be an earnest desire, an intense longing, that God will supply this need. There must be readiness of heart and mind to act on faith, in harmony with whatever God may require. Finally, there must be willingness to order the life henceforth in harmony with the principles of the kingdom of heaven, and to bear witness to the love and power of God." SDA Bible Commentary vol. 5 p. 209, 210

It is note worthy to point out here that miracles as valuable as they are, do not give the strongest evidence of the genuineness of the gospel. It is said that "the highest evidence that He came from God is that His life revealed the character of God. He did the works and spoke the words of God. Such a life is the greatest of all miracles." "A consistent life in Christ is a great miracle. In the preaching of the word of God, the sign that should be manifest now and always is the presence of the Holy Spirit, to make the word a regenerating power to those that hear. This is God's witness before the world to the divine mission of His Son." Desire of Ages 407

Throughout His earthly ministry Jesus exercised authority that amazed his followers. It was such authority that led the disciples to cry our "what manner of man is this?" This authority, however, had been voluntarily limited. Now once more he possesses all the authority He had before he laid it down to come in rescue of mankind. With full authority Christ commissioned His disciples "go ye." This command does not end with the first disciples to whom it was spoken. Christ included all those who will come unto Him through the preaching of the Gospel to the end of time. Just as the eleven were learners in the school of Christ before being sent, Christians must learn of Christ through the teaching of the Word and personal relation with Him before they can be representatives of His divine grace.

The work of the gospel must go forward in the power and the authority that Christ Himself gave. As the gospel is presented in every land, disciples will be born who will take their stand with those who are active in His work to reach every people, tongue and nation of the earth. Christianity is the first religion with a true international character.

The gospel commission is purely a mission of peace making. It eliminates national boundaries, and people from all nations become members of one great family where "there is neither Jew nor Greek, there is neither bond nor free, there is neither male nor female," for all are "one in Christ Jesus."

> Christianity effectively destroys all barriers of race, nationality, society, economics, and social custom. Christianity depends for success on its disentanglement from all national peculiarities, forms of government, social institutions, and everything of a purely local character. SDA Bible Commentary vol. 5 p. 557

This world-wide mission of peace will not be accepted by all men nevertheless, the disciple of Christ will proclaim the message as a witness to all men. All who believe and accept the gospel shall be saved and those who chose not to believe will receive condemnation. God will bless His work with supernatural and miraculous demonstrations of His divine power and authority.

Never alone, no never alone; the peace maker has the divine team of Father, Son and Holy Spirit on his side. He stands in the three-fold authority of 1) the name of Jesus—every tongue shall confess that Jesus is Lord. 2) In the all powerful blood of Jesus and 3) on the authority given to him in the word of God. With such divine power and authority may every disciple arise, take up the work that has been assigned him and go forth into the world of sin, sadness and death, a world in which the prince of darkness claim legal rights over the lives of men—and set captives free.

CALLS FOR LABORERS

A spirit of worldliness and selfishness has deprived the church of many a blessing. We have no right to suppose an arbitrary withholding from the church of the divine light and power, to account for its limited usefulness. The measure of success which in the past has followed well-directed effort contradicts such as idea. Success has ever been granted proportionate to the labor performed. It is the limitation of labors and sacrifices alone which as restricted the usefulness of the church. The missionary spirit is feeble; devotion is weak; selfishness and cupidity, covetousness and fraud, exist in its members.

Does not God care for these things? Can He not read the intents and purposes of the heart? Earnest, fervent, contrite prayer would open to them the windows of heaven and bring down showers of grace. A clear, steady view of the cross of Christ would counteract their worldliness and fill their souls with humility, penitence, and gratitude. They would then feel that they are not their own, but that they are the purchase of Christ's blood.

A deadly spiritual malady is upon the church. Its members are wounded by Satan; but they will not look to the cross of Christ, as the Israelites looked to the brazen serpent, that they may live. The world has so many claims upon them that they have not time to look to the cross of Calvary long enough to see its glory or to feel its power. When they now and then catch a glimpse of the self-denial and self-dedication which the truth demands, it is unwelcome, and they turn their attention in another direction, that they may the sooner forget it. The Lord cannot make His people useful and efficient while they are not careful to comply with the conditions He has laid down.

Great demands are everywhere made for the light which God has given to His people; but these calls are for the most part in vain. Who fells the burden of consecrating himself to God and to His work? Where are the young men who are qualifying themselves to answer these calls? Vast territories are opened before us where the light of truth has never penetrated. Whichever way we look we see rich harvests ready to be gathered, but there are none to do the reaping. Prayers are offered for the triumph of the truth. What do your prayers mean, brethren? What kind of success do you desire?—A success to suit your indolence, your selfish indulgence?—A success that will sustain and support itself without any effort on your part?

There must be a decided change in the church which will inconvenience those who are reclining on their lees, before laborers who are fitted for their solemn work can be sent into the field. There must be an awakening, a spiritual renovation. The temperature of Christian piety must be raised. Plans must be devised and executed for the spread of truth to all nations of the earth. Satan is lulling Christ's professed followers to sleep while souls are perishing all around them, and what excuse can they give to the Master for their negligence?

The words of Christ apply to the church: "Why stand ye here all the day idle?" Why are you not at work in some capacity in His vineyard? Again and again He has bidden you: "Go ye also into the vineyard; and whatsoever is right, that shall ye receive." But this gracious call from heaven has been disregarded by the large majority. Is it not high time that you obey the commands of God? There is work for every individual who names the name of Christ. A voice from heaven is solemnly calling you to duty. Heed this voice, and go to work at once in any place, in any capacity. Why stand ye here all the day idle? There is work for you to do, a work that demands your best energies. Every precious moment of life is related to some duty which you owe to God or to your fellow men, and yet you are idle!

A great work of saving souls remains yet to be done. Every angel in glory is engaged in this work, while every demon of darkness is opposing it. Christ has demonstrated to us the great value of souls in that He came to the world with the hoarded love of eternity in His heart, offering to make man heir to all His wealth. He unveils before us the love of the justifier of him that believeth.

"Christ pleased not Himself." He did nothing for Himself; His work was in behalf of fallen man. Selfishness stood abashed in His presence. He assumed our nature that He might suffer in our stead. Selfishness, the sin of the world has become the prevailing sin of the church. In sacrificing Himself for the good of men, Christ strikes at the root of all selfishness. He withheld nothing, not even His own honor and heavenly glory. He expects corresponding self-denial and sacrifice on the part of those whom He came to bless and save. Everyone is required to work to the extent of his ability. Every worldly consideration should be laid aside for the glory of God. The only desire for worldly advantages should be that we may the better advance the cause of God.

Christ's interests and those of His followers should be one; but the world judge that they are separate and distinct, for those who claim to be Christ's pursue their own ends as eagerly, and waste their substance as selfishly, as non-professors. Worldly prosperity comes first; nothing is made equal to this. The cause of Christ must wait till they gather a certain portion for themselves. They must increase their gains at all hazards. Souls must perish without a knowledge of the truth. Of what vale is a soul for whom Christ died in comparison with their gains, their merchandise, their houses and lands? Souls must wait till they get prepared to do something. God calls these servers of Mammon slothful and unfaithful servants, but Mammon boasts of them as among his most diligent and devoted servants. They sacrifice their Lord's goods to ease and enjoyment. Self is their idol.

Suppose Christ should abide in every heart and selfishness in all its forms should be banished from the church, what would be the result? Harmony, unity, and brotherly love would be seen as verily as in the church which Christ first established. Christian activity would be seen everywhere. The whole church would be kindled into a sacrificial flame for the glory of God. Every Christian would cast in the fruit of his self-denial to be consumed upon the altar. There would be far greater activity in devising fresh methods of usefulness and in studying how to come close to poor sinners to save them from eternal ruin.

The third angel of Revelation 14 is represented as flying swiftly through the midst of heaven crying: "Here are they that keep the commandments of God, and the faith of Jesus," Here is shown the nature of the work of the people of God. They have a message of so great importance that they are represented as flying in the presentation of it to the world. They are holding in their hands the bread of life for a famishing world. The love of Christ constraineth them. This is the last message. There are no more to follow, no more invitations of mercy to be given after this message shall have done its work. What a trust! What a responsibility is resting upon all to carry the words of gracious invitation: "And the Spirit and the bride say, Come. And let him that heareth say, Come. And let him that thirst come. And whosoever will, let him take the water of life freely."

Everyone who heareth is to say: Come. Not only the ministers, but the people. All are to join in the invitation. Not only by their profession, but by their character and dress, all are to have a winning influence. They are made trustees for the world, executors of the will of One who has bequeathed sacred truth to men. Would that all could feel the dignity and glory of their God-given trust. *(Testimonies for the Church p. 202-207)*

Peace-makers are often misunderstood. The judgment of others so quickly is pronounced upon their service of love. Like the early disciples the floods of persecution may come from every direction. This in no way brings discouragement to peace-makers for they have learn to rejoice even in persecution. They count it all joy to share in the suffering of their Saviour.

CHAPTER NINE

---•---

REJOICE WHEN PERSECUTED

Key 8

Persecution for righteousness sake

Fellowship with God awakens the enmity of the world. Thus Christians share in the reproach of Christ. They now travel the path that has been treaded by the noblest of the earth. They meet persecution with rejoicing. Each fiery trial is God's agent for their refinement. Each is preparing them for their work as laborers with Him. Every conflict has its place in the great battle for righteousness, and each will add to the joy of their final triumph.

B lessed are they which are persecuted for righteousness' sake: for theirs is the kingdom of heaven. Blessed are ye, when men shall revile you, and persecute you, and shall say all manner of evil against you falsely, for my sake. Rejoice, and be exceeding glad: for great is your reward in heaven: for so persecuted they the prophets which were before you. Matthew 5: 10-12

To be persecuted is to endure suffering for Christ, to be mocked, ridiculed, criticized, and ostracized; to be treated with hostility; to be martyred.

Christ is here speaking primarily of persecution suffered in the course of forsaking the world for the acceptance of the Kingdom of heaven. Christ does not give His disciples the hope of walking with Him without self-denial and reproach. Jesus made it clear that persecution awaits all those who follow Him. He says:

> But previous to all this, they will lay their hands on you and persecute you, turning you over to the synagogues and prisons, and you will be led away before kings and governors for My name's sake. This will be a time (an opportunity) for you to bear testimony. Resolve and settle it in your minds not to meditate and prepare beforehand how you are to make your defense and how you will answer. For I [Myself] will give you a month and such utterance and wisdom that all of your foes combined will be unable to stand against or refute. You will be delivered up and betrayed even by parents and brother and relatives and friends, and [some] of you they will put to death. And you will be hated (despised) by everyone because [you bear] My name and for its sake. But not a hair of your head shall perish. By your steadfastness and patient endurance you shall win the true life of your souls. Luke 21: 12-19 Amp.

Peter an apostle of Jesus Christ admonished the saints by saying:

> Beloved, do not be amazed and bewildered at the
> fiery ordeal which is taking place to test your quality,
> as though something strange (unusual and alien to
> you and your position) were befalling you. If you are
> censured and suffer abuse [because you bear] the name
> of Christ, blessed [are you—happy, fortunate, to be
> envied, with life—joy, and satisfaction in God's favor
> and salvation, regardless of your outward condition],
> because the Spirit of glory, the Spirit of God, is resting
> upon you. On their part He is blasphemed, but in your
> part He is glorified. 1 Peter 4: 12, 14 Amp.

In the passage under consideration Christ makes mention of three
major kinds of persecution:

1. Being reviled, meaning to reproach, to slander, to insult.

Jesus says in Luke 6:22—

> Blessed . . . are you when people despise (hate) you,
> and when they exclude and excommunicate you [as
> disreputable] or revile and denounce you and defame
> and cast out and spurn your name as evil (wicked) on
> account of the Son of Man. Amp.

Excommunication might be either permanent, involving complete
exclusion from Judaism for all time, or merely temporary. In the time
of Christ temporary excommunication lasted for a period of thirty
days, during which the person thus "separated" was not only deprived
of participation in religious ritual, but was not supposed to come
within 4 cub. (about 7 ft.) of another person. Excommunication thus

implied booth religious and social contamination, or uncleanness. (See Jerusalem Talmud Moed Katan 3.81c. 50, cited in SDA Bible Commentary vol. 5 p. 747 from Strack and Billerbeck, Kommentar zum Neuen Testatment, Vol. 4 p. 299)

Reproach means to revile, to heap insults upon someone. It is very common for persecutors to begin their work by slandering the integrity, intelligence and conduct of the Christian as a citizen. Reproach is an introduction to more cruel attacks by persecutors.

2. Persecuted—hurt, ostracized, attacked, tortured, martyred, and treated with hostility.

Paul said of his own life, of the Jews five times received I forth stripes save one. Thrice was I beaten with rods, once was I stoned, thrice I suffered shipwreck, a night and a day I have been in the deep. (2 Corinthians 11: 24, 25)

3. All manner of evil spoken against you:

—slandered, cursed, lied about, "hard speeches" harsh defiant words.

Psalms 35:11 states:

False witnesses did rise up; they laid to my charge things that I knew not. (KJV)

Acts 17:6-7—* *shows the attitude of those who are against the will of God.*

But when they failed to find them, they dragged Jason and some of the brethren before the city authorities, crying, these men who have turned the world upside down have come here also, and Jason has received them to his house and privately protected them! And they are all ignoring and acting contrary to the decrees of Caesar, [actually] asserting that there is another King, one Jesus!

The disciples maintained their obedience to their master, even though it was disobedience to local authorities. In this case those who helped the disciples were physically mistreated.

"He who came to redeem the lost world was opposed by the united forces of the adversaries of God and man. In an unpitying confederacy, evil men and evil angels arrayed themselves against the Prince of Peace. Though His every word and act breathed of divine compassion; His unlikeness to the world provoked the bittersweet hostility. Because He would give no license for the exercise of the evil passions of our nature, He aroused the fiercest opposition and enmity. So it is with all who will live godly in Christ Jesus. Between righteousness and sin, love and hatred, truth and falsehood, there is an irrepressible conflict. When one presents the love of Christ and the beauty of holiness, he is drawing away the subjects of Satan's kingdom, and the prince of evil is aroused to resist it. Persecution and reproach await all who are imbued with the Spirit of Christ. The character of the persecution changes with the times, but the principle—the spirit that underlies it—is the same that has slain the chosen of the Lord ever since the days of Abel. Thought From the Mount of Blessing 29

Whenever men turn from the world and its follies and pursue a course to come into harmony with God, they will discover that the offense of the cross is still evidently alive. Principalities and powers and evil spirits in high places will come against all who will walk in obedience to the law of heaven. Persecution, however, instead of bringing grief should bring joy to the heart of Christ's disciples, for it gives evidence that they are following in the steps of their Lord and Master.

Nowhere in His Word does God promise an exemption from trials and persecution. He promised, however, that which is exceedingly better.—strength for every experience.

> Your castles and stronghold shall have bars of iron and bronze, and as your day, so shall your strength, your rest and security, be. (Deut. 33:25)
>
> My grace (My favor and loving-kindness and mercy) is enough for you [sufficient against any danger and enables you to bear the trouble manfully]; for My strength and power are made perfect (fulfilled and completed) and show themselves most effective in [your] weakness. Therefore, I will all the more gladly glory in my weakness and infirmities, that the strength and power of Christ (the Messiah) may rest (yes, may pitch a tent over and dwell) upon me! 2 Cor. 12:9 Amp.

God's answer to Paul is interesting—"My grace is sufficient for thee,"—this phrase is in the emphatic position. Paul's prayer did not produce the release from his affliction but it made available to him enough grace to endure it. Paul's request for deliverance from his infirmity was doubtlessly on the ground that it was an obstruction to his ministry. In response, Christ met his need with a profuse supply of grace. It is not the promise of God to modify situations or even liberate men from trouble. To God, physical infirmities and inconvenient circumstances are themes of secondary importance. Inward strength to endure the circumstances is of far greater manifestation of divine grace than the working of outward difficulties of life. In spite of the outward state, it is the privilege of the child of God, inwardly to enjoy perfect peace.

If you are called to go through the fiery furnace for the sake of the name of Christ, go knowing and believing that Jesus will be right there by your side. This was the living experience of three young men in Babylon.

> Then these [three] men were bound in their cloaks, their tunics or undergarments, their turbans, and their other clothing, and they were cast into the midst of the burning fiery furnace. Therefore because the King's commandment was urgent and the furnace was exceedingly hot, the flame and sparks from the fire killed those men who handled Shadrach, Meshach, and Abednego.
>
> Then Nebuchadnezzar the King [saw and] was astounded, and he jumped up and said to his counselors. Did we not cast three men bound into the midst of the fire? They answered, True, O King. He answered, Behold, I see four men loose, walking in the midst of the fire, and they are not hurt! And the form of the fourth is like a son of the gods! Then Nebuchadnezzar came near to the mouth of the burning fiery furnace and said, Shadrach, Meshach, and Abednego, you servants of the Most High God, come out and come here. Then Shadrach, Meshach, and Abednego, came out from the midst of the fire. Daniel 3: 21, 22, 25, 26.

The true children of God will rejoice in every opportunity to share in the reproach and humiliation of Jesus. The power of the love they have for Him makes suffering for His sake acceptable.

History shows that in all periods of time the people of God have been persecuted by Satan. They were tortured in many different ways and put to death. "They revealed in their steadfast faith a mightier One than Satan. Satan could torture and kill the body, but he could not touch the life that was hid with Christ in God. He could incarcerate in prison walls, but he could not bind the spirit." Thought from the Mount of Blessing 31

[But what of that?] For I consider that the suffering of this present (this present life) are not worth being compared with the glory that is about to be revealed to us and in us and for us and conferred on us! Romans 8: 18 Amp.

For our light, momentary affliction (this slight distress of the passing hour) is ever more and more abundantly preparing and producing and achieving for us an everlasting weight of glory [beyond all measure, excessively surpassing all comparisons and all calculations, a vast and transcendent glory and blessedness never to cease!] 2 Corinthians 4: 17 Amp.

How comforting to know that our light affliction is only for a moment. Compared with eternity, a moment is nothing at all. The child of God can afford to endure affliction for a brief space of time—a moment. Paul said that affliction pursued him every day, and everywhere he went. Focusing on them by themselves his affliction was weighty and intense, but when compared to eternity and all that it has in store, they were just a momentary experience.

Affliction adds to our eternal glory by purifying, refining and elevating our character. Behold, I have refined you, but not as silver; I have tried and chosen you in the furnace of affliction. Isa. 48:10. Hebrews puts it this way:

And have you [completely] forgotten the divine word of appeal and encouragement in which you are reasoned with and addressed as sons? My son, do not think lightly or scorn to submit to the correction and discipline of the Lord, nor lose courage and faint when you are reproved or corrected by Him, for the Lord corrects and disciplines everyone whom He loves, and He punishes, even scourges, every son whom He accepts and welcomes to His heart and cherishes. You must submit to and endure [correction] for discipline; God is dealing with you as with sons. For what son is there whom his father does not [thus] train and correct and discipline? Now if you are exempt from correction and left without discipline in which all [of God's children] share, then you are illegitimate offspring and not true sons [at all]. Moreover, we have had earthly fathers who disciplined us and we yielded [to them] and respected [them for training us]. Shall we not much more cheerfully submit to the Father of Spirits and so [truly] live? For [our earthly fathers] disciplined us for only a short period of time and chastised us as seemed proper and good to them; but He disciplines us for our certain good; that we may become sharers in Him own holiness. For the time being no discipline brings joy, but seems grievous and painful; but afterwards it yields a peaceable fruit of righteousness to those who have been trained by it [a harvest of fruit that consists in righteousness—in conformity to God's will in purpose, thought, and action, resulting in right living and right standing with God]. Hebrews 12: 5-11 Amp.

Affliction exercises a restraining influence upon the heart and mind. It levels pride, suppresses self, and is repeatedly the means of brining the believers will into complete harmony with the will of God. Through it, the faith of the believer, is tested and the authenticity of his profession as a Christian. Affliction creates circumstances for the perfection of faith, for faith becomes strong by exercise. It aids the believer to perceive things in their true point of view and to put the most important things first. Affliction creates in the children of God appropriateness for glory. When the intentions of the world are confiscated through the discipline of suffering, Christians will find it painless to set their affections on the things of heaven. "If then you have been raised with Christ [to a new life, thus sharing His resurrection from the dead], aim at and seek the [rich, eternal treasures] that are above, where Christ is, seated at the right hand of God, and set your minds and keep them set on what is above the higher things), not on the things that are on the earth." (Colossians 3:1-2) Afflictions take us into difficult situations where we learn to distrust our own wisdom, recognize our helplessness and our total need of God. "Again, they are diminished and brought low through oppression, affliction and sorrow." (Ps.107:39) Sorrow, trial and suffering contribute to our understanding of our fellow men and for us developing feelings of compassion toward them.

Trials and persecution are tools that reveal the character of God in His people. Though hated and persecuted by the world, the children of God receive their discipline and education in the school of their Master. Their purification comes from time spent in the furnace of affliction. They walk looking to Christ through conflicts, self-denial and experiencing bitter disappointments. Their painful experience teaches them the woefulness of sin. As partakers of the suffering of Christ, they are appointed to be partakers of His divine glory. John on the Island of Patmos says:

And I saw as it were a sea of glass mingled with fire: and them that had gotten the victory over the beast, and over his image, and over his mark, and over the number of his name, stand on the sea of glass, having the harps of God. And they sing the son of Moses the servant of God and the song of the Lamb, saying, Great and marvelous are thy works, Lord God Almighty; just and true are thy ways, thou King of Saints. (Rev. 15:2-3 KJV)

I replied, Sir, you know. And he said to me, these are they who have come out of the great tribulation (persecution), and have washed their robes and made them white in the blood of the Lamb. For this reason they are [now] before the [very] throne of God and serve Him day and night in His Sanctuary (temple); and He Who is sitting upon the throne will protect and spread His tabernacle over and shelter them with His presence. Rev. 7:14, 15 Amp.

"There was never one who walked among men more cruelly slandered than the Son of Man. He was derided and mocked because of His unswerving obedience to the principles of God's holy laws. They hated Him without a cause. Yet He stood calmly before His enemies, declaring that reproach is a part of the Christian's legacy, counseling His followers how to meet the arrows of malice, bidding them not to faint under persecution." Thought from the Mount of Blessing 33

Our reputation may be blackened with gossip and slander, however shameful it seems, it cannot taint the character. There is no power, whether Satanic or human that can stain the soul as long as we refuse to sin. "A man whose heart is stayed upon God in just the same in the hour of his most afflicting trials and most discouraging surrounding as when he was in prosperity, when the light and favor of God seemed to be upon him." (Ibid) When his actions, words and motives are misrepresented, he does not mind or seek to justify himself for he has far greater interests at stake.

> Since we consider and look not to the things that are seen but to the things that are unseen; for the things that are visible are temporal (brief and fleeting), but the things that are invisible are deathless and everlasting. 2 Corinthians 4: 18

The child of God waits patiently on Him. He remains calm. Trusting in the promises of Him who cannot lie; for there is no secret that shall not be made known, and those who honor God shall be honored by Him before angels and men.

> "In every age God's chosen messengers have been reviled and persecuted, yet through their affliction the knowledge of God has been spread abroad. Every disciple of Christ is to step into the ranks and carry forward the same work, knowing that its foes can do nothing against the truth, but for the truth." Ibid. 34

Heaven now holds in reserve a great reward for those who are witnesses for Christ through trial, persecution and reproach. Christ does not place it all in the future life, for it begins right here and now.

In Genesis 15:1 the word of the Lord to Abram was: fear not, Abram, I am your Shield; your reward shall be exceedingly great.

This is the reward of all who follow Christ:

> In Him, all the treasures of [divine] wisdom
> (comprehensive insight into the ways and purposes of
> God) and [all the riches of spiritual] knowledge and
> enlightenment are stored up and lie hidden. Col. 2:3
> Amp.

In Christ, in His office and function, in His person and ministry, in the fact that He is both Son of God and Son of man, are embedded the details of the mystery of God. He is the source as He is the treasure house of the blessings of God." "In Christ may be discovered all that God purposes to reveal in blessing for humanity." "Jesus is the mine from which all true riches come. To those who receive Him, He gives truth in its fullness . . . . In Christ, the living Word resides the essential knowledge." (SDA Bible Commentary vol. 7 p. 200) To receive Jesus is to receive the source of all that's needed for this life and the hereafter.

> For in Him the whole fullness of Deity (the
> Godhead) continues to dwell in bodily form [giving
> complete expression of the divine nature]. Col. 2:9 Amp.

The sum total of the nature and attributes of God dwells in Christ. The powers of Deity inhabit Him continually. All the fullness of the Father is revealed in Him. Everything that God is, every feature of Deity—"dignity, authority, excellency, power in creating and fitting the world, energy in upholding and guiding the universe, love in redeeming mankind, forethought in supplying everything needful for each of His creatures" Ibid—reside in Christ bodily.

To receive Christ is to be brought into sympathy with Him, to know Him, to possess Him, as the heart opens more and more to receive His attributes: to know His love and power, to possess the unsearchable riches of Christ, to comprehend more and more:

That you may have the power and be strong to apprehend and grasp with all the saints [God's devoted people, the experience of that love] what is the breadth and length and height and depth [of it]; [that you may really come] to know [practically, through experience for yourselves] the love of Christ, which far surpass mere knowledge [without experience]; that you may be filled [through all your being] unto all the fullness of God [may have the richest measure of the divine Presence, and become a body wholly filled and flooded with God Himself]! Eph. 3:18, 19 Amp.

Christ is the reward of His people. All that He is, He is for and too His people. When Christ dwells in the heart of His people, they share in His Divinity.

Isaiah 54:17 says:

But no weapon that is formed against you shall prosper, and every tongue that shall rise against you in judgment you shall show to be in the wrong. This [peace, righteousness, security, triumph over opposition] is the heritage of the servants of the Lord [those in whom the ideal servant of the Lord is reproduced]; this is the righteousness or the vindication which they obtain from Me [this is that which I impart to them as their justification], says the Lord. Amp.

It is the promise of God to care for His own and to vindicate them before their enemies. No evil man, not even demons will be able to prevail against them. When the enemy seeks to fight against His people, God will declare them innocent and deliver them. When tackled by forbidding circumstances in which it seems that injury and suffering is about to be experienced at the hand of persecutors, the children of God can join the psalmist by saying, "The Lord is on my side; I will not fear: what can man do unto me?" (Ps. 118:6)

This was the Joy that flooded the hearts of Paul and Silas when at midnight they prayed and sang praises to God in the Philippians dungeon. The light of the presence of Christ radiated the prison with glory from above. Paul unmindful of his chains wrote from Rome, "I therein do rejoice, yea, and will rejoice." Philippians 1:18 He wrote to the Philippian church in the midst of their persecutions—Rejoice in the Lord always [delight, gladden yourselves in Him]; again I say, Rejoice! (Phil. 4:4)

There is much that can be learned from the faithfulness of Stephen.

"Because the priests and rulers could not prevail against the clear, calm wisdom of Stephen, they determined to make an example of him; and while thus satisfying their revengeful hatred, they would prevent others through fear, from adopting his belief. Witnesses were hitred to bear false testimony that they had heard him speak blasphemous words against the temple and the law. "We have heard him say," these witnesses declared, "that this Jesus of Nazareth shall destroy this place, and shall cjange the customs which Moses delivered us."

As Stephen stood face to face with his judges to answer to the charge of blasphemy, a holy radiance shone upon his countenance, and "all that sat in the council, looking steadfastly on him, saw his face as it had been the face of an angel." Many who beheld this light trembled and veiled their faces, but the stubborn unbelief and prejudice of the rulers did not waver." The Acts of the Apostles p. 98-99

After presenting the eight keys to progressive spiritual development, Jesus stated to His disciples, "Ye are the light of the world. A city that is set on a hill cannot be hid." Matthew 5: 14

CHAPTER TEN

THE LIGHT OF THE WORLD

I n relation to light the Bible has this to say of the eternal God. "Who alone has immortality [in the sense of exemption from every kind of death] and lives in unapproachable light, Whom no man has ever seen or can see. 1 Timothy 6: 16 Amp.

Light is the full outshining of Deity, for John declares: And this is the message [the message of promise] which we have heard from Him and now are reporting to you: God is Light, and there is no darkness in Him at all [no, not in any way]. 1 John 1: 5 Amp.

God lives in unapproachable light, for He Himself is light. Light is the symbol and expression of holiness.

In Him who is the light there is no darkness—which is the universal symbol and condition of sin and death. It is clear from scripture that God is the source of light. Without Him there is no light or life. This brings us to the question of who is Jesus in relation to the light.

In John 1: 1 **He is the eternal Word** (logos)
In the beginning was the Word, and the Word was with God, and the Word was God.

He is the sole expression of the glory of God [the Light-being, the out-raying or radiance of the divine], and He is the perfect imprint and very image of [God's] nature, upholding and maintaining and guiding and propelling the universe by His mighty word of power . . . Hebrews 1: 3 Amp.

The light of men
There it was—the true light [was than] coming into the world [the genuine, perfect, steadfast Light] that illumines every person. John 1: 9

The light to the Gentiles
I the Lord have called You [the Messiah] for a righteous purpose and in righteousness; I will give you for a covenant to the people [Israel], for a light to the nations [Gentiles] Isaiah 42: 6 Amp.

Light of the world
Once more Jesus addressed the crowd. He said, I am the Light of the world. He who follows Me will not be walking in the dark, but will have the Light which is Life. John 8: 12
As long as I am in the world, I am the world's Light. John 9: 5
I have come as a Light into the world, so that whoever believes in Me [whoever cleaves to and trust in and relies on Me] may not continue to live in darkness. John 12: 46 Amp.

God manifest in the flesh
And great and important and weighty, we confess, in the hidden truth (the mystic secret) of godliness. He [God] was made visible in human flesh, justified and vindicated in the [Holy] Spirit, was seen by angels,

preached among the nations, believed on in the world, [and] taken up in glory. 1 Timothy 3: 16 Amp.

As logos (the Word), Jesus is the eternal expression of God. Let us consider the threefold essence of His being.

1. God is Life (Zoe)

    For even as the Father has life in Himself and is self-existent, so He has given to the Son to have life in Himself and be self-existent. John 5: 26 Amp.

    Just as the living Father sent Me and I live by (through, because of) the Father, even so whoever continues to feed on Me [whoever takes Me for his food and is nourished by Me] shall [in his turn] live through and because of Me. John 6: 57 Amp.

2. God is Love (agape)

    He who does not love has not become acquainted with God [does not and never did know Him], for God is love. 1 John 4: 8 Amp.

3. God is Light (phos)

    God is Light, and there is no darkness in Him at all [no, not in any way]. 1 John 1: 5 Amp.

Christ the logos is thus the manifestation of the threefold aspects of the Divine Nature, Life, Love and Light. These three aspects are inseparable and constitute the glory which was seen in Him; "and we [actually] saw His glory (His honor, His majesty), such glory as an only begotten son receives from his father, full of grace (favor, loving-kindness) and truth." John 1: 14 Amp.

Christ is the light of men because he reveals and gives life. God gives His glory through him: For God who said, Let light shine out of darkness, has shone in our hearts so as [to beam froth] the Light for the illumination of the knowledge of the majesty and glory of God [as it is manifest in the Person and is revealed] in the face of Jesus Christ (the Messiah). 2 Corinthians 4: 6 Amp

Those who catch and reflect the light of Christ are called lights.

John was the lamp that kept on burning and shining [to show you the way], and you were willing for a while to delight (sun) yourselves in his light. John 5: 35 Amp.

Christ calls those who follow Him children of light.

While you have the light, believe in the light [have faith in it, hold to it, rely on it], that you may become sons of the Light and be filled with Light . . . John 12: 36 Amp.

For once you were darkness, but now you are light in the Lord; walk as children of Light [lead the lives of those native-born to the Light]. Ephesians 5: 8 Amp.

Those who follow Christ are expected to be seen as lights in the world.

That you may show yourselves to be blameless and guileless, innocent and uncontaminated, children of God without blemish (faultless, unrebukable) in the midst of a crooked and wicked generation [spiritually perverted and perverse], among whom you are seen as bright light (stars or beacons shining out clearly) in the [dark] world. Philippians 2: 15 Amp.

Let us consider some of the things in scripture that light are a symbol of:

1. The Eye

The light of the body is the eye: if therefore thine eye be single, thy whole body shall be full of light. But if thine eye be evil, the whole body shall be full of darkness. If therefore the light that is in thee be darkness, how great is that darkness? Matthew 6: 22-23 KJV (see Luke 11: 34)

In verse 22 the word light comes from the Greek word *"luchnos"* meaning *"lamp"* and not from *phos*, light.

"Luchnos refers to the source of light or to the medium through which it shines, not to the light itself. Verse 22 and 23 provide an illustration of the principle stated in vs. 19-21. Excessive concern for the accumulation of worldly wealth is evidence of defective spiritual eyesight, of darkness in the soul. The light of the body is that insight that places a true relative value on the things of time and of eternity.

"A Christian whose spiritual "eye" is "single," or "sound," is one whose insight and judgment make him a man of unaffected simplicity, artless, plain, and pure. He sees the things of time and eternity in true perspective.

"Singleness of eyesight results in singleness of purpose, in wholehearted devotion to the kingdom of heaven and to the practice of its eternal principles. To be effective, vision must be focused and concentrated. In the same way, the man who desires true light in his soul must have his spiritual eyesight in sharp focus. Otherwise his vision will be blurred and his estimation of truth and duty will be faulty. SDA Bible Commentary vol. 5 p. 350

2. Watchfulness

Keep your loins girded and your lamps burning.
Luke 12: 35

Here we have the sense of urgency. The Christian is called to be always ready for action. Watchfulness becomes the keynote of his life. In view of the eminent return of the Master, all those who are bearers of the light will make right living their priority.

3.   Protection

> The night is far gone and the day is almost here.
> Let us then drop (fling away) the works and deeds of
> darkness and put on the [full] armor of light. Romans
> 13: 12 Amp

Paul contrasts here the present life to that which is to come as night and day. He counsels the believers to throw away all the clothing that must be taken off. In it place the Christian is to adorn himself with armor of righteousness and truth, that he may be ready for the coming of his Lord. This armour of light is design to be in contrast wwith the works of darkness. Thus Christians are called "out of darkness into his marvelous light" (1 Peter 2:9). They are called "children of light" (1 Thess. 5:5) and therefore fight the spiritual battle with weapons of light—their only protection.

4.   Christian Daily Walk

> Giving thanks to the Father, who has qualified
> and made us fit to share the portion which is the
> inheritance of the saints (God's holy people) in the
> Light. Colossians 1: 12 Amp.

In our main passage, Christ Jesus says to his disciples, "you are the light of the world." We have seen above that God is the source of light. He who was in the beginning with God, the Word who is God Himself, came into the world to be the light-bearer. He who is the Light of men now says to His people, you are the light. Having accepted Jesus Christ as the light of the world, Christians become reflectors of Christ's light. We do not become the source of light but reflectors of the light. Just as the moon has no light in itself but reflects the light of the sun, so the Christian has no light of himself but reflect the light of the Son of God.

When the lives of men are illumine by the true Light, the light beams out dispelling darkness and is seen by the world.

Arise [from the depression and prostration in which circumstances have kept you—rise to a new life]! Shine (be radiant with the glory of the Lord), for your light has come and the glory of the Lord has risen upon you! For behold, darkness shall cover the earth, and dense darkness [all] peoples, but the Lord shall arise upon you [O Jerusalem], and His glory shall be seen on you. And nations shall come to your light, and kings to the brightness of your rising. Isaiah 60: 1-3 Amp.

Those who love and serve the Lord Jesus Christ are pictured as the sun in this life and in the kingdom to come.

Then will the righteous (those who are upright and in right standing with God) shine forth like the sun in the Kingdom of their Father. Matthew 13: 43 Amp

Citizens of the Kingdom of Christ are to go forth and let their light shine abroad in this dark and wicked world, dispelling the darkness of sin and ignorance of the will and ways of the God of heaven.

The purpose of every light-bearer is to proclaim the praises of God.

But you are a chosen race, a royal priesthood, a dedicated nation [God's] own purchased, special people, that you may set forth the wonderful deeds and display the virtues and perfections of Him who called you out of darkness into His marvelous light. 2 Peter 1: 9 Amp.

As the light of the world, citizens of the Kingdom have a responsibility to:

1. Be Visible

   The world must see and take notice of the children of God by what they do. Jesus said to His disciples—By this shall all [men] know that you are

My disciples, if you love one another [if you keep on showing love among yourselves] John 13: 35 Amp.

2. Be Radiant

Dearly beloved, I beseech you as strangers and pilgrims, abstain from fleshly lusts, which war against the soul, having your conversation honest among the Gentiles: that, whereas they speak against you as evildoers, they may by your good works, which they shall behold, glorify God in the day of visitation. 1 Peter 2: 11-12

3. Be Guides

Men and women must be led to Jesus—I am come a light into the world, that whosoever believeth on me shall not abode in darkness. John 12: 46

Spiritual darkness had for a long time clouded the souls of men, but now the true light of life and perfection shines to brighten the pathway of every man. Not only does this light shine through Christ, He is the light. "As the first act of creation God flooded the world with light, so when God sets about the work of recreating His image in the souls of men He first illumines their hearts and minds with the light of divine love." SDA Bible Commentary vol. 5 p. 898

"God is light, and in the words "I am the light of the world," Christ declared His oneness with God and His relation to the whole human family. It was He whom at the beginning had caused "the light to shine out of darkness." (2 Cor. 4: 6) He is the light of sun and moon and star. He was the spiritual light that in symbol and type and prophecy had shone upon Israel. But not to the Jewish nation alone was the light given. As the sunbeams penetrate to the remotest corners of the earth, so does the light of the Sun of Righteousness shine upon every soul.

"That was the true light which lighteth every man that cometh into the world." The world has had its great teachers, men of giant intellect and wonderful research, men whose utterances have stimulated though, and opened to view vast fields of knowledge; and these men have been honored as guides and benefactors of their race. But there is one who stands higher than they." As many as received Him, to them gave He power to become the sons of God. No man hath seen God at any time; the only-begotten Son, which is in the bosom of the Father, He hath declared Him. (John 1: 12, 18). We can trace the line of the worlds great teachers as far back as human records extend; but the Light was before them. As the moon and the stars of the solar system shines by the reflected light of the sun, so, as far as their teaching is true, do the world's great thinkers reflect the rays of the Sun of Righteousness. Every gem of thought, every flash of the intellect, is from the Light of the world. In these days we hear much about "higher education." The true "higher education" is that imparted by Him "in whom are hid all the treasures of wisdom and knowledge." "In Him was life; and the life was the light of men."(Col. 2: 3; John 1: 4). He that followeth Me, said Jesus, "shall not walk in darkness, but shall have the light of life."

Just as the sun goes out each morning on its mission of love, eliminating the darkness of the night and introducing the world to life, Christ's followers are to go into the world diffusing heavens light upon those in darkness of error and sin.

"Satan has ever sought to misrepresent the Father. Christ cam to dispel the darkness and to reveal the Father. This same work Christ committed to His disciples. Light shines, not so much that men may see the light, as that they may see other things because of the light. Our light are to shine, not so that men may be attracted to us, but that they may be attracted to Christ, who is the light of life, and to things worth while." SDA Bible Commentary vol.5 p. 331)

Christians are called to be more than light among men. We are the light of the world—of men. To all who comes to Christ, He says, you have given yourself to Me, and I have given you to the world as My representatives. Jesus said in John 17: 18, "just as you sent me into the world, I also have sent them into the world." (When we give ourselves to Jesus we no longer have control or authority over ourselves. We become His to do with us what He pleases—we do whatever He wants us to do.) Just as Christ is the revelation of the Father, so we are called and sent into the world to be the revelation of Christ.

Jesus our Master is the source of light and this light is revealed to the world through humanity. God uses human instrumentality to bestow His blessings. Christ came to this world as the son of man. In Him, humanity was united to the divine nature in order to touch humanity. In the church of God upon the earth, every individual disciple is heavens appointed channel for the revelation of God to mankind. Heavenly angels stand ready and waiting to communicate through you—Christ's disciples—heaven's light and power, to souls that are ready to die. If the appointed agents fail in the accomplishing of his work, the world will be robbed of the promised influence of the Holy Spirit.

The command of Jesus to His disciples here is not "strive to make your light shine," or "try to make your light shine." He said, "let your light shine,"—let it shine. If the presence of Christ is dwelling in the heart, it will be impossible to conceal the light of His presence. If the profess disciples, of Christ are not the light of the world, it is so because the needed power has left them. If there is no light to give, it is because there is no connection with the Source of light.

Whenever the Spirit of God inhabited His people, He has made them the light of the people of that generation. Today, the Disciples of Christ are light bearers, through whom the mercy and goodness of God are made manifest to the world enshrouded in the darkness of misapprehension of God. By the display of their good works prompted by the Holy Spirit men are led to glorify the Father in heaven. Men are made to take notice of the divine love glowing in the heart, the Christ-like harmony manifested in the life. These are like glimpses of heaven given to men of the world so that they may appreciate its excellence. Men are thereby led to believe in the love God has toward His people.

And we know (understand, recognize, are conscious of, by observation and by experience) and believe (adhere to and put faith in and rely on) the love God cherishes for us. God is love, and he who dwells and continues in love dwells and continues in God, and God dwells and continues in him. 1 John 4: 16 Amp.

The heart that was once sinful and corrupt are now purified and transformed, that Jesus can make a joyous presentation of it to God:

Now to Him Who is able to keep you without stumbling or slipping or falling and to present [you] unblemished (blameless and faultless) before the presence of His glory in triumphant joy and exultation [with unspeakable, ecstatic delight] Jude 24 Amp.

"The Saviors words, "ye are the light of the world," point to the fact that He has committed to His followers a world-wide mission. In the days of Christ, selfishness and pride and prejudice had built strong and high the wall of partition between the appointed guardians of the sacred oracles and every other nation on the globe. But the savior had come to change all this. The words which the people were hearing from His lips were unlike anything to which they had ever listened from priest or rabbi. Christ tears away the wall of partition, the self-love, the dividing prejudice of nationality, and teaches a love for all the human family. He lifts men from the narrow circle that their selfishness prescribes; He abolishes all territorial lines and artificial distinctions of society. He makes no difference between neighbors and strangers, friends and enemies. He teaches us to look upon every needy soul as our neighbor and the world as our field.

"As the rays of the sun penetrate to the remotest corners of the globe, so God designs that the light of the gospel shall extend to every soul upon the earth. If the church of Christ were fulfilling the purpose of our Lord, light would be shed upon all that sit in darkness and in the region and shadow of death. Instead of congregating together and shunning responsibility and cross bearing, the members of the church would scatter into all lands letting the light of Christ shine out of them, working as He did for the salvation of souls and this "gospel of the kingdom" would speedily be carried to all the world." Thoughts From the Mount of Blessing p. 42-43.

The message of Christ as delivered through the gospel prophet, which are reechoed in the Sermon on the Mount, are for us in this final generation. "Arise [from the depression and prostration in which circumstances have kept you—rise to a new life]! Shine (be radiant with the glory of the Lord), for your light has come, and the glory of the Lord has risen upon you! Isa. 60: 1 Amp.

Has the glory of the Lord risen upon your spirit? Have you been afforded the privilege to behold the beauty of Him who is the chiefs among ten thousand—the one altogether lovely? Has your soul become lighted with the presence of His glory? To you who are walking in this experience with the Savior, this word from the Master is sent. Have you been on the mount of transfiguration with Christ? Do not remain there, for down in the plain there are souls enslaved by Satan who are waiting for the word of faith and prayer to set them free.

Can you by faith understand the wonderful plan of redemption, behold the glory of the only-begotten Son of God, and not speak of it? Can you ponder the unfathomable love that was manifested on the cross of Calvary in the death of Christ, that you might have eternal life and still have no words to extol the saviors' glory?

The cross of Calvary is to be lifted high above the people, absorbing their minds and concentrating their thoughts. Then all the spiritual faculties will be charged with divine power direct from God. Then there will be a concentration of the energies in genuine work for the Master. The workers will send forth to the world beams of light, as living agencies to enlighten the earth. Thoughts from the Mount of Blessing 44

Today, right now, Christ will accept you gladly, if you will totally surrender to Him. He will create a union of the human with the divine, so that He may communicate to the world around you the mysteries of incarnate love. "Trials patiently borne, blessings gratefully received, temptations manfully resisted, meekness, kindness, mercy, and love habitually revealed, are the lights that shine forth in the character in contrast with the darkness of the selfish heart, into which the light of life has never shone." Thoughts from the Mount of Blessing 44

SUMMERY

---◆---

The Beatitudes

"And seeing the multitudes, he went up into a mountain; and when he was set, his disciples came unto him." As far as possible we should try to bring before us the scene of our Saviour's labors, that we may fasten our attention upon the occasion of the lessons which our Lord addressed to the people. The words of our lesson are from the lips of no other than the Majesty of heaven. They are not the words of man, that may be criticised, but are the words of Him who was equal with the Father, one with God. In these words we recognize the voice of the highest authority that ever spake to man.

"And he opened his mouth, and taught them, saying, Blessed are"—those who are filled with joyful emotion? who are highly elated? who feel that they are rich in spiritual attainment?—No; "Blessed are the poor in spirit; for theirs is the kingdom of heaven." Do you ask what it means to be poor in spirit? The next verse is of a like character, and says, "Blessed are they that mourn; for they shall be comforted." To be poor in spirit means that we feel our deficiency and need because we have sinned and come short of the glory of God. It is this that causes us to mourn. But because the Saviour says, "Blessed are they that mourn," are we to come to the conclusion that he would have us always lamenting our poverty of spirit, our lack of spiritual grace? Is it necessary to make it manifest that you are mourning, in order to be counted among those whom the Saviour pronounces "blessed"?—No; for by beholding we become changed, and if we talk of our poverty and weakness, we shall only become more poverty-stricken, more feeble in spiritual things. If we talk darkness, we shall have darkness. To be poor in spirit is to be never satisfied with present attainments in the Christian life, but to be ever reaching up for more and more of the grace of Christ. The poor in spirit is one who looks upon the perfection of Jesus' character, and sees his own unlikeness to him who is glorious in holiness. The poor in spirit is one who is ever responding to the drawing of Christ, and who is obtaining nearer and nearer views of the perfect righteousness of Christ, and in contrast sees his own unworthiness and unlikeness to his Lord.

He is poor in spirit, but he is not making a parade of his poverty; he shows that he is of this class by manifesting humility and meekness, by not depreciating others that he may exalt himself. He has no time for doing this; he sees many defects in his own character which demand his attention, and he knows that he cannot afford to be found criticising others. As he beholds the infinite love and mercy of God towards sinners, his heart is melted. He feels his poverty of spirit, but instead of calling attention to his weakness he seeks continually for the richness of the grace of Christ, for the robe of his righteousness. The language of the heart of him who is poor in spirit is, "Less of self and more of Thee." He desires Jesus. He knows that there is nothing in him whereby he can procure the freedom which Christ has purchased for him at the infinite price of his precious blood. He sees that the good works which he has done are all mingled with self, and he can take no glory to himself because of his attainments in the Christian life. He realizes that there is merit in naught else but the blood of Christ. But it is because of this very realization that he is blessed; for if he did not feel his need, he would not obtain the heavenly treasure.

When Christ was upon earth, the Pharisees made bitter complaint against him because he was the friend of publicans and sinners. They said to his disciples: "Why eateth your Master with publicans and sinners? But when Jesus heard that, he said unto them, They that be whole need not a physician, but they that are sick." The Pharisees felt that they were whole; they felt that they were rich and increased with goods and had need of nothing, and knew not that they were poor and miserable and blind and naked and wretched. They were satisfied with their moral condition, but Jesus said, "I am not come to call the righteous, but sinners to repentance." It is the needy that Jesus is seeking. Brethren and sisters, do you feel that you are needy? Are you saying, as did the Greeks that came to Jerusalem, "We would see Jesus"? The Greeks came to seek Jesus at the time when the Pharisees were upon his track, trying by every possible way to find something whereby they could accuse and condemn him. How grateful to the Master was the sincere desire and confidence of the Greeks at this time of trial and sorrow. The Greeks wanted to see him because they had heard of his mighty works, they had heard of his wisdom and truth, and they believed on him; for they knew that he was the desire of their hearts.

The great danger with the people who profess to believe the truth for this time is that they shall feel as if they were entitled to the blessing of God because they have made this or that sacrifice, done this or that good work, for the Lord. Do you imagine that because you have decided to keep the Sabbath of the Lord, God is under obligation to you, and that you have merited his blessing? Does the sacrifice you have made look of sufficient merit to you to entitle you to the rich gifts of God? If you have an appreciation of the work that Christ has wrought out for you, you will see that there is no merit in yourself or in your work. You will see your lost condition and become poor in spirit. There is but one thing for the poor in spirit to do, and that is to look continually to Jesus, to believe in him whom the Father hath sent.

When the people came to Jesus, they asked him at one time: "What shall we do, that we might work the works of God? Jesus answered and said unto them, This is the work of God, that ye believe on him whom he hath sent." Now the question is, Are we doing this? Do we feel our need? God has committed to us sacred trusts. The hereditary trusts of patriarchs and prophets have come down along the lines to us, and with them precious light has shone upon us. We have received divine enlightenment, and yet we have not made the advancement in the pathway of holiness that we should have made. Our obligation and responsibility have been faithfully pointed out, but we have not taken hold upon the strength of God, that we might fulfill our obligations to him. Throughout all the churches there is one subject of vital importance that has been neglected. We have failed to make the Holy Spirit the theme of our thought and instruction. Light has come to us concerning the offices of the Spirit of God, and with burdened heart some have presented to the church the great provision that God has made for the people in the gift of his Holy Spirit.

Jesus said to his disciples: "It is expedient for you that I go away; for if I go not away, the Comforter will not come unto you; but if I depart, I will send him unto you. And when he is come, he will reprove the world of sin, and of righteousness, and of judgment." The Comforter is to come as a reprover, as one who is to lay open before us our defects of character, and at the same time to reveal to us the merit of Him who was one with the Father. Jesus says, "He shall glorify me; for he shall receive of mine, and shall show it unto you." In Christ dwelt all the fullness of the God-head bodily, and we are to be complete in him. With all our defects of character, we are to come to him in whom all fullness dwells.

But many of you say, "I have prayed, I have tried, I have struggled, and I do not see that I advance one step." What is the trouble? Have you not thought you were earning something, that you were by your struggles and works paying the price of your redemption? This you never can do. Christ has paid the price of your redemption. There is only one thing that you can do, and that is to take the gift of God. If you feel that you are poverty-stricken in spirit, you can come in all your need, and plead the merits of a crucified and risen Saviour. But you cannot come expecting that Christ will cover your wickedness, cover your indulgence in sin, with his robe of righteousness. He has come to save his people from their sins. The people of God are to be as branches grafted into the living Vine, to be partakers of the nature of the Vine. If you are a living branch of the True Vine, Jesus will prove you by affliction, that you may bring forth fruit more abundantly.

The reason why we have not more of the Spirit and power of God with us is that we feel too well satisfied with ourselves. There is a marked tendency among those who are converted to the truth, to make a certain measure of advancement, and then settle down into a state of solidity, where no further progress is attained. They stand right where they are, and cease to grow in grace and in the knowledge of our Lord and Saviour Jesus Christ. But the religion of Christ is of a character that demands constant advancement. The Lord does not design that we shall ever feel that we have reached to the full measure of the stature of Christ. Through all eternity we are to grow in knowledge of him who is the head of all things in the church. If we would draw upon his grace, we must feel our poverty. Our souls must be filled with an intense longing after God, until we realize that we shall perish unless Christ shall put upon us his Spirit and grace, and do the work for us.

But as we come to feel our utter reliance upon Christ for salvation, are we to fold our hands and say, I have nothing to do, Jesus has done it all?—No; we are to put forth every energy, that we may become "partakers of the divine nature, having escaped the corruption that is in the world through lust." We are to be overcomers, to overcome the world, the flesh, and the devil. We are to be continually watching, waiting, praying, and working. But do all that we may, yet we can do nothing to pay a ransom for our souls. But while we see our helplessness, we are to be continually looking unto Jesus, who is the

Author and Finisher of our faith. We can do nothing to originate faith, for faith is the gift of God. Neither can we perfect it, for Christ is the Finisher of our faith. It is all of Christ.

All the longing after a better life is from Christ, and is an evidence that he is drawing you to himself and that you are responding to his drawing power. You are to be as clay in the hands of the potter, and if you submit yourself to Christ, he will fashion you into a vessel unto honor, fit for the Master's use. The only thing that stands in the way of the soul who is not fashioned after the divine Pattern is that he does not become poor in spirit; for he who is poor in spirit will look to a higher Source than himself, that he may obtain the grace which will make him rich unto God. While he will feel that he cannot originate anything, he will say, "The Lord is my helper."

The Lord has commanded us, "Work out your own salvation with fear and trembling." But what does this mean? It means that you feel your necessity that you are poor in spirit that you rejoice with trembling. It means that you know that in the very words you utter you may make a mistake that in the very best of your work self may be so mingled that your efforts may be valueless, that you realize that your efficiency is in Christ. Oh, let the cry of the soul continually be—"Hangs my helpless soul on Thee."

Look to Jesus when you come in and when you go out, and pray without ceasing. You should realize that temptation is on every side. Around you are those whose conversation is only chaff and nonsense. In the world pride and vanity are displayed, and you will be tempted to feel poverty concerning these things that the world admires, which can never satisfy the soul's hunger. Oh, then pray, "Lord, make me a jewel for thy kingdom."!

This is the meaning of working out your salvation with fear and trembling. If you do not work out your salvation in this spirit, your righteousness is of as much worth as was the Pharisee's who went into the temple to pray, who exalted and extolled himself, and thanked the Lord that he was not as other men were. He was rich in spirit, or thought that he was; for he knew not that he was poor, and miserable, and blind, and naked. But at the same time a poor publican entered the temple, and he would not so much as lift up his eyes to heaven, but smote upon his breast, and cried, "Lord, be merciful to me a sinner." The Pharisee saw this man, and thanked God that he was not as this publican, and he went down to his house feeling satisfied with himself-feeling rich in spirit and lifted up in spiritual pride. But he who had so exalted himself in his own eyes was not exalted in the sight of God, for Jesus says that the publican went down to his house justified rather than the other.

"Blessed are the poor in spirit; for theirs is the kingdom of heaven." The humility that Jesus speaks of in the text is not a humility on stilts, as was the Pharisee's, parading itself before the eyes of men, that his righteousness might be seen and praised of men. Humility is before honor. The apostle exhorts the followers of Christ: "Humble yourselves in the sight of the Lord, and he shall lift you up." "Work out your own salvation with fear and trembling." Fear lest you shall make a mistake, and bring dishonor upon the name of the Lord. Cry unto him, believing that he has power to save. This is the humility that we want. We need a physician and restorer for our souls, and when we come unto Christ petitioning for his grace, the Comforter will breathe his words into our souls, "My peace give I unto you." "Blessed are the poor in spirit; for theirs is the kingdom of heaven." We are to come as little children to God; and as we realize our poverty, we are not to tell it to men, but to God. Do not tell your weakness to those who can give you no strength. Tell it to God; for he will know just what to do for you. Jesus said: "The Spirit of the Lord God is upon me; because the Lord hath anointed me to preach good tidings unto the meek; he hath sent me to bind up the broken-hearted, to proclaim liberty to the captives, and the opening of the prison to them that are bound; . . . to comfort all that mourn; to appoint unto them that mourn in Zion, to give unto them beauty for ashes, the oil of joy for mourning, the garment of praise for the spirit of heaviness; that they might be called trees of righteousness, the planting of the Lord that he might be glorified."

How thankful we should be that we have a heavenly Intercessor. We may be clothed in Christ's righteousness, that the Father may bestow his favor upon us. Jesus presents us to the Father robed in his righteousness. He pleads before God in our behalf. He says" "I have taken the sinner's place. Look not upon this wayward child, but look on me. Look not upon his filthy garments, but look on my righteousness." When we are forgiven for our sins, when our filthy garments are taken away, then we are to work out our salvation with fear and trembling; but we are not left to do the work alone, "for it is God that worketh in you both to will and to do of his good pleasure." God works and man works, and as this co-operation is maintained, the richest blessings will come upon those who labor together with God. The Lord says, "To this man will I look, even to him that is poor and of a contrite spirit, and trembleth at my word." "For thus saith the high and lofty One that inhabiteth eternity, whose name is Holy: I dwell in the high and holy place, with him also that is of a contrite and humble spirit, to revive the spirit of the humble, and to revive the heart of the contrite ones." "Blessed are the poor in spirit; for theirs is the kingdom of heaven."

"Blessed are they that mourn; for they shall be comforted." But although the Lord says the mourner shall be comforted, it is not that he shall exalt himself as did the Pharisee. He who has mourned for his sin knows that there is nothing in him whereby he has merited the returns that God has bestowed. He beholds in Jesus "the Chiefest among ten thousand" and "the One altogether lovely," and he centers his affections upon Christ. If Jesus were the center of attraction to you, the One on whom your affections were placed, would you hide this love in your heart, and never let it out?—No; you would tell of his love, you would catch his spirit, and imitate his example.

"Blessed are the meek; for they shall inherit the earth." But the earth promised to the meek will be a better one than this. It will be purified from all sin and defilement, and will bear the image of the divine. Satan has placed his throne in the earth; but Jesus says where the usurper has set up his throne, there will I place my throne, and there shall be no more curse. The glory of the Lord is to cover the earth as the waters cover the sea. Jesus is working for us. He desires to give his children a home where there will be no more sin, no more sorrow, no more death; but all will be joy and gladness. He says: "The wilderness and the solitary place shall be glad for them, and the desert shall rejoice, and blossom as the rose. It shall blossom abundantly, and rejoice even with joy and singing; the glory of Lebanon shall be given unto it, the excellency of Carmel and Sharon; they shall see the glory of the Lord, and the excellency of our God."

The Lord desires to take every son and daughter of Adam, and purify them from their iniquity, and lift them up from their state of misery and degradation and wretchedness, and write upon them his divine superscription. But it is man's sin and unbelief that oppose the work that God would do for humanity. Jesus died for the whole world, but in stubborn unbelief men refuse to be fashioned after the divine pattern. They will not yield themselves to Christ to be molded after the heavenly model. Oh, shall we not submit, and give up our own way, that the Lord may have a chance to do the work for us?

How tenacious are men of their own way. They try to excuse their sinful habits by saying, "Oh, this is my way." But will your way be acceptable to God? Will you present your way at the gate of the city into which nothing that defileth shall enter, and expect to have an entrance there? The Lord will say: "I know your way, and it is a wicked way. You would not permit me to rule over you on earth, and you are not prepared for an entrance here. You refused to be led by my spirit, you rejected my counsel, and set at naught my grace, and heaven would not be heaven to you, for nothing that defileth can enter here. We emptied sin from heaven when we cast out the great deceiver, and we cannot have sin here again." Then let us yield our wills to God that he may mold and fashion us after the Divine Pattern.

How blessed will be the lot of those who enter into that glorious abode where there will be no more sin, no more suffering. What a prospect is this for imagination. What a theme for contemplation. The Bible is full of the richest treasures of truth, of glowing descriptions of that heavenly land. We should search the Scriptures, that we may better understand the plan of salvation, and learn of the righteousness of Christ, until we shall exclaim in viewing the matchless charms of our Redeemer, "Thy gentleness hath made me great." In the word of God we shall see the infinite compassion of Jesus. The imagination may reach out in contemplation of the wonders of redeeming love, and yet in its highest exercises we shall not be able to grasp the height and depth and length and breadth of the love of God, for it passeth knowledge. In Christ was the fullness of the Godhead bodily. In him every treasure of heaven was given, and he has it in trust for us. Oh, then why do we not trust him? Why do we doubt his tender mercy and love? Do you think that He who died for you, cares not whether you are saved or not? Do you imagine that he cares not for the bereaved, the mourning ones that he looks not with pity on the poor in spirit, who are under the bondage of Satan? The tender, compassionate Jesus, who died for the sins of the world, will not turn away from the cry of the needy. He asks: "Can a woman forget her sucking child, that she should not have compassion on the son of her womb? yea, they may forget, yet will I not forget thee. Behold I have graven thee upon the palms of my hands; thy walls are continually before me."

Jesus invites the needy to come to him and find completeness in him who is the fullness of the Godhead bodily. The Saviour of men designs to cleanse his children until no particle of selfishness shall remain. While we feel our poverty, we are to eat of the flesh and drink of the blood of the Son of God. We are to co-operate with Christ in working out our own salvation with fear and trembling. The heavenly intelligences are waiting to co-operate with the most helpless, the most sinful soul who feels his need. Those who are great sinners may find great grace.

Jesus said to Simon, "I have somewhat to say unto thee. And he saith, Master, say on. There was a certain creditor which had two debtors; the one owed five hundred pence, and the other fifty. And when they had nothing to pay, he frankly forgave them both. Tell me therefore, which of them will love him most? And Simon answered and said, I suppose that he to whom he forgave most. And he said unto him, Thou hast rightly judged . . . . To whom little is forgiven, the same loveth little."

In view of our weakness, how does it become us to indulge in criticism of others? Do not fault-finding and picking flaws in the character of those with whom you associate make it evident that you are stricken with spiritual poverty? You are feeding on the faults of others, instead of growing in grace and in the knowledge of our Lord and Saviour Jesus Christ. We are to be laborers together with him in bringing souls to the knowledge of the truth. But we must not expect that souls are to be converted simply by hearing a sermon. We are to bring them one by one to Christ, and all that have ever tasted of the good word of God and of the powers of the world to come are to be missionaries for God. When you become engaged in the work of Christ, seeking to bring in those who are lost, you will not have time to look for the defects in the character of your brethren. You must now build yourselves up in the most holy faith, lifting up holy hands without wrath and doubting. You are not to stand to one side as a spectator, looking on to see what this one or that one is doing; your business is to see that you are making straight paths for your feet, that the lame be not turned out of the way. When a follower of Christ turned to one of his brethren and asked, "Lord, what shall this man do?" Jesus answered, "What is that to thee? Follow thou me." The follower of Christ is not to look to any man. He is to look to a crucified and risen Saviour.

"Blessed are they which do hunger and thirst after righteousness; for they shall be filled." All through this Sermon on the Mount is a line of advancement for Christian experience. The angels of darkness are to stand back, that the soul purchased by the infinite sacrifice of Christ may attain unto perfection of character. The word is sounded: "Stand back, this soul is not yours, it has been purchased by the precious blood of Christ. Stand back, I and my Father are one, and we have come to draw this soul to righteousness." If the soul is not drawn to Christ, it is because the will is not on the side of God's will, but on the side of the enemy. If man will but cooperate with God, God will work in him to will and to do of his good pleasure, and man will work out his own salvation with fear and trembling. The reason you do not realize the help of the Lord to a far greater degree is that you are so self-centered, your will is not on the side of God's will. The Lord would have you make it manifest in your manners, in your dress, in your spirit, that you are blessed. He would have you show that the line of demarkation between the world and the followers of Christ is a distinct line, so decided that the difference between him that serveth God and him that serveth Him not is always discernible. If the people of the world do not see that you are different from those around them, they will not be influenced by your profession of religion; for you will not be a savor of Christ, and you will win no soul to the service of God.

Yet there will be no one saved in heaven with a starless crown. If you enter, there will be some soul in the courts of glory that has found an entrance there through your instrumentality. Then why not entreat the Lord to put upon you His Spirit, that you may be able to awaken an interest in the truth in the minds of those around you? Think of your neighbors and friends and relatives who are out of Christ. Think of those you have left in various foreign lands; how much do you care for their souls? You should be so filled with love for the lost that you cannot forbear working for the salvation of souls. What you need is Jesus. He says, "Whosoever drinketh of the water that I shall give him shall never thirst; but the water that I shall give him shall be in him a well of water springing up into everlasting life." If the rich blessing of Jesus is in your hearts, you will be able to refresh others.

How many have their names upon the church books who know not what it means to have Christ abide in their hearts by faith. There are many who make a profession of Christianity who will have to be born again or they cannot see the kingdom of heaven. They will have to become partakers of his love and grace before they can present to others the great salvation that has been provided for those who are dead in trespasses and sins. But the promise is given to those who feel their want, "Blessed are they which do hunger and thirst after righteousness; for they shall be filled." God has promised the fullness of salvation, and yet the world is full of those who are hungering and thirsting after the pleasures, the fashions, the applause of the world. Many are hungering and thirsting, that they may have their own way. But those who are hungering and thirsting after righteousness are directing their desires along the channel where the fullness of heaven shall be given. Why not determine that you will place your will on the side of God's will, that you may become a laborer together with God. Jesus says, "Ye shall receive power, after that the Holy Ghost is come upon you; and ye shall be witnesses unto me." Then is there any excuse for our weakness, for our coldness, for our lethargy? There are many who seem to think that when they have acknowledged that they are full of weakness, they have put a plaster over their sins. But we are not to talk of our inefficiency, but to find in Christ a full salvation. He says, "Him that cometh unto me I will in nowise cast out."

When our weakness becomes strength in the strength of Christ, we shall not be craving for amusement. These holidays that are considered so indispensable will not be used simply for the gratification of self, but will be turned into occasions in which you can bless and enlighten souls. When weary, Jesus sought for a place of rest in the desert, but the people had had a taste of the heavenly manna, and they came out to him in large companies. In all their human woe and suffering and distress, they sought his retreat, and there was no rest for the Son of God. His heart was moved with compassion, for they were as sheep without a shepherd, and his great heart of love was touched with the feeling of their infirmities, and he taught them concerning the kingdom of heaven.

Jesus has presented to us precious truth full of spiritual light and vitality. But has this truth been brought into the inner sanctuary of the soul? Does Christ abide in your hearts by faith? If Christ is in you, you will make him manifest to others. We must have more of Jesus, and less, far less, of self. The prayer of our hearts should be, "As the hart panteth after the water brooks, so panteth my soul after thee, O God." Jesus must abide in the heart; and where he is, the carnal desires will be subdued and be kept in subjection by the operation of the Spirit of God. "For the weapons of our warfare are not carnal, but mighty through God to the pulling down of strongholds; casting down imaginations, and every high thing that exalteth itself against the knowledge of God, and bringing into captivity every thought to the obedience of Christ."

I feel like mourning that the image of Christ is not clearly discernible in those who profess to be his followers; for I know that Jesus is disappointed, that the heavenly intelligences are disappointed, and those who are seeking for the truth are disappointed. Unless Christ is formed within, the hope of glory, you cannot rightly represent him to those with whom you come in contact.

"Blessed is He That Considereth the Poor."

The Lord Jesus said, "Blessed are the merciful; for they shall obtain mercy." There never was a time when there was greater need for the exercise of mercy than today. The poor are all around us, the distressed, the afflicted, the sorrowing, and those who are ready to perish. Those who have acquired riches have acquired them through the exercise of the talents that were given them of God; but these talents for the acquiring of property were given to them that they might relieve those who are in poverty. These gifts were bestowed upon men by Him who maketh His sun to shine and His rain to fall upon the just and the unjust, that by the fruitfulness of the earth men might have abundant supplies for all their need. The fields have been blessed of God, and "of his goodness he hath prepared for the poor." In the providence of God events have been so ordered that the poor are always with us, in order that there may be a constant exercise in the human heart of the attributes of mercy and love. Man is to cultivate the tenderness and compassion of Christ; he is not to separate himself from the sorrowing, the afflicted, the needy, and the distressed. Job declares: "When the ear heard me, then it blessed me; and when the eye saw me, it gave witness to me; because I delivered the poor that cried, and the fatherless, and him that had none to help him. The blessing of him that was ready to perish came upon me; and I caused the widow's heart to sing for joy."

How many there are who claim to be followers of Christ, yet who do not follow him in truth. They do not manifest the sympathy and love of Christ by being merciful and compassionate. They do not make the widow's heart sing for joy; they treat the fatherless with coldness, indifference, or contempt. Said Job: "I put on righteousness, and it clothed me; my judgment was as a robe and a diadem; I was eyes to the blind, and feet was I to the lame. I was a father to the poor; and the cause which I knew not I searched out." This was an evidence that Job had righteousness that was after Christ's order. Through Jesus men may possess a spirit of tender pity toward the needy and distressed. They may have the mind of Christ. He was the Son of God, rich in heavenly treasures, yet for our sake he became poor, he descended to the lowest humiliation and was obedient unto death, even the death of the cross, that he might exalt us to be joint heirs with himself. The whole world was in need of that which Christ alone could give them. He did not withdraw himself from those who called upon him for help. He did not do as many now do, say, "I wish they would not trouble me with their affairs, I want to hoard up my means, to invest it in houses and lands." Jesus, the Majesty of heaven, turned from the splendor of his heavenly home, and in the gracious purpose of his heart he demonstrated the character of God to men throughout the world. The requirement of God from those who claim to be his children is that they be doers of his word, that they follow his example, represent the life of Christ in tender, pitying love to the world; that they reflect his image.

Jesus says, "Be ye therefore merciful, as your Father which is in heaven is merciful." To pursue the course that Jesus did, to follow in his divine footsteps, is not in harmony with the feelings of the natural heart; but if we are Christians, we shall practice the words and works of Christ, who gave himself in order to ransom an apostate race. The root of selfishness has a firm growth in many hearts, and worldliness and pride spring from this root; but selfishness is not a Christian characteristic; it is an attribute of the great apostate. No one can live for himself and at the same time be united with Christ. Conformity to the world, attachment to the world, manifests a decided denial of Christ.

The rich are not to be favored above the poor. How inconsistent is it to make favorites of men because the Lord has intrusted his goods to them to be wisely dispensed to those who are needy. Unless the rich manifest the spirit that moved Christ to come to our world to seek and to save that which was lost, they are none of his. They are training under another general. The important question is not, "Is a man rich?" But the important question is, "What use does he make of his riches?" The value and character of a man is determined by the use to which he puts his intrusted talents. Does he do good in this life? Does he seek to bless humanity, to build up the kingdom of Christ in the world? Shut away the rich from the poor in large and costly dwellings, make churches too splendid for the entrance of the poor, so that the rich man may not be brought in contact with the distressing needs of the fatherless and the widow, and the result will be that his sympathies will be withered, mercy will not be exercised, and the rich man will be in imminent danger of losing his soul.

Christ says, "How hardly shall they that have riches enter into the kingdom of God." Unless the grace of Christ controls the heart, the tendency of the rich man is to grow more proud, more self-sufficient, more self-righteous. He acts as if he were made of better flesh and more costly blood than his poorer brother. But Christ looks on, and says, "All ye are brethren." There is no respect of persons with God. The rich man has plenty, and makes no effort to put himself in the poor man's place; but because he does not consider the poor, he becomes unfeeling, indifferent, and hard-hearted. He does not try to understand the conflicts, temptations, and struggles of his poor brethren, and mercy dries up in his heart.

The poor are robbed daily of the education and training they should have concerning the tender mercies with which the Lord would have them regarded; for he has made ample provision that they should be comforted with the necessities of life. They are compelled to feel the poverty that narrows life, and they are often tempted to become envious, jealous, and full of evil surmisings. Their sympathies are alienated from their more prosperous neighbors; but when men are born again, when they are truly converted, old things pass away, and behold, all things become new. A new moral taste is created, and he that was exalted because God had intrusted him with means will seek to aid and exalt others. His responsibilities will seem weighty upon him and will humble his heart before God; for he will realize that his goods are intrusted of the Lord, that he may relieve the needy, comfort the distressed, feed the fatherless, and make the widow's heart sing for joy.

But instead of using their means for the Master, how many embezzle it, invest it for themselves, furnishing their homes with rich carpets, fine furniture, and multiplying lands and houses to glorify themselves in the earth, while the needy call upon them in vain. If they do anything for the poor, they call them paupers, and look upon them with contempt. They do not consider from whence comes their intrusted capital, and that they are all the time receiving unnumbered blessings from God. If he should withhold his beneficence, they would be numbered with the poor. We are all dependent upon the benevolence of a gracious God. The day will come when those who have cherished selfishness and covetousness, who have defrauded the poor, who have withdrawn mercy and love from them, will be made manifest.

"Blessed is He that Considereth the Poor."

God has placed property in the hands of men in order that they may learn to be merciful, to be his almoners to relieve the suffering of his fallen creatures. Further than this, they are to consider the wants of the cause of God, and keep his treasury supplied according to the gifts bestowed upon them. Satan has had power to make men haughty and like himself in character, so that the money given them of God has been used for the gratification of self, and the cry of the poor has reached unto God against them; for they have been unmerciful in their conduct toward the needy. Whatever we spend for that which is not necessary for health and godliness will be charged as robbery against God; because all that was spent for the gratification of self someone needed to obtain necessary food and clothing.

Those who have the Spirit of Christ will see all men through the eyes of divine compassion. No matter what may be the social position, no matter what his wealth or how high his education, if a man is in Christ, he will not be unkind, uncourteous, hard-hearted, and merciless. Since every soul is entirely dependent upon God for every blessing he enjoys, how patient, how merciful, we should be to every creature. God looked upon man in his lost condition, in his degradation and guilt, and paid the same price for the ransom of the poor and the outcast that he paid to ransom the rich with all his intrusted talents. There is no respect of persons with God. All are candidates for heaven or hell. All need to be taught every hour of God, to be diligent students, that in their time they may make a wise use of their intrusted ability, that they may be living agencies to cooperate with the heavenly intelligences for the saving of men's souls, that with tender hearts, overflowing with mercy and true goodness, they may work as Christ worked. The apostle says, "Ye are laborers together with God." You are to look after the poor you are to look after the fatherless ones, who need your wisdom, your care, your love, and help. You are to look after the widow. You are to look after those who go in want, in hunger, in rags, who are depraved in principle; for Jesus came to seek and to save that which is lost. God cares for the outcast, and do you think yourself too good, too honorable, to bear the yoke with Christ, in seeking to save the perishing? Will you despise your fellow-men? Will you become an offense to God by slighting and despising His image in man? In distinct lines Christ has revealed the relation of man to his fellow-man. Jesus, the only-begotten Son of God, has settled that question forever in the example he has set to the world. Ask yourself: Am I my brother's keeper? And who is my neighbor?

There is in society an increasing tendency to separate the rich from the poor, to set them apart in distinct, definite classes; but this is not at all after God's order, but after the policy of Satan. Heaven looks with pain and amazement upon the scenes that are daily enacted among those who are called Christians. Many cannot read the meaning of the great plan of redemption because Satan has cast his shadow upon their pathway. Many who could be as lights in the world, as the salt of the earth, who command great resources for doing good to their fellow-men, are not in union and sympathy with Christ, that they may be laborers together with God. They have felt that a high value was set upon them, that they were placed above their brethren, and even above their own flesh and blood. They have expended their Lord's goods in lifting up their souls unto vanity, in cultivating pride, envy, self-exaltation. They have surrounded themselves with costly luxuries, and placed themselves in a position which it was impossible for their brethren to reach, and they have left the poor in their poverty to get along as they could without sympathy and love. God looks down from heaven, and hates all these pretensions. He calls for men who have intellect, men who have property, men who have moral worth, to change this order of things.

Let every leader of the people associate with the people; for they really need his help, so that sympathy shall not congeal in the human breast.

No church should become so lifted up that its members shall feel above the poor, and the poor feel that they cannot enter freely into the house of God. A church that is too rich for the poor to feel at home in is too aristocratic for Jesus to make one in its assembly. This narrow exclusiveness that shuts man away from his brother is an abomination in the sight of God. When men are converted, they will have an abiding sense of the fact that they have been bought with a price. Whatever may be the sum of our talents, whether one, two, or five, not a farthing of our money is to be squandered upon vanity, pride or selfishness. Every dollar of our accumulation is stamped with the image and superscription of God. As long as there are hungry ones in God's world to be fed, naked ones to be clothed, souls perishing for the bread and water of salvation, every unnecessary indulgence, every overplus of capital, pleads for the poor and the naked. It is no light thing to be intrusted with riches, although men treat their position and property as though they were not accountable to any one, as though it was by their own virtue that they had these things. "How hardly shall they that have riches enter into the kingdom of God." Those who consecrate themselves to God, with their riches, becoming laborers together with him, are the only ones to whom the King of glory will give the benediction: "Come, ye blessed of my Father, inherit the kingdom prepared for you from the foundation of the world." "Well done, thou good and faithful servant, thou hast been faithful over a few things, I will make thee ruler over many things."